The Life of ⌐ . . . , . . .

ABBOT OF THE MONASTERY

AT

WEARMOUTH AND JARROW

BY AN UNKNOWN AUTHOR

OF THE EIGHTH CENTURY

TRANSLATED FROM THE ORIGINAL, AND EDITED

(WITH INTRODUCTORY ESSAY AND NOTES)

BY

DOUGLAS SAMUEL BOUTFLOWER, M.A.

LATE SCHOLAR OF CAIUS COLLEGE, CAMBRIDGE,

AND CHANCELLOR'S ENGLISH MEDALLIST,

SOMETIME VICAR OF MONKWEARMOUTH

Now first Published in English

TO WHICH IS ADDED A REPRINT OF AN

ARTICLE ON THE CODEX AMIATINUS

BY THE LATE REV. J. L. LOW

(Church Quarterly Review)

Facsimile reprint 1991 by Llanerch Press.
ISBN 0947992 61 8.
First published in 1912 (Sunderland, & London).

ADVERTISEMENT TO THE READER.

THE Life of Ceolfrid (whose name should be pronounced as Cholfrid) dates from the early part of the eighth century. It is the production of a monk of the monastery of Wearmouth and Jarrow, whose identity is unknown.

The Latin text followed is that of the Rev. Charles Plummer, Fellow of Corpus Christi College, Oxford—Clarendon Press, 1896, Vol. I. pp. 388-404. Certain suggested emendations will be found in the notes of this volume, pp. 89-92.

Where, as occasionally happens, the original gives variant spellings of proper names, the form first occurring has been repeated throughout the work.

D. S. BOUTFLOWER.

Christ Church Vicarage,
Bishopwearmouth,
September, 1912.

CONTENTS.

quia inpotestate erat !
sermo ipsius.
et insynagoga erat homo haben
daemonium inmundum
et exclamauit uoce magna
dicens : -
sine quid nobis et tibi ihu
nazarene uenisti perderen
scio te qui sis scs di.
et increpauit illi ihs dicens
ommutesce et exi ab illo.
et cum proiecisset illud
daemonium inmedium
exiit ab illo nibilque.
illum nocuit.
et factus est pauor in omnib'
et conloquebantur
ad inuicem dicentes
quod est hoc uerbum
quia inpotestate et uirtute
imperat spiritibus
inmundis et exeunt.
et diuulgabatur fama de illo

A portion of a page from

THE CODEX AMIATINUS,

in the Laurentian Library, Florence.

INTRODUCTION.

THE purpose of this small volume is to bring
to the notice of English readers the anonymous
work of the early part of the eighth century
conventionally known since its first publication
as *The Lives of the Abbots of Wearmouth and
Jarrow*. This description is unfortunately both
confusing and incorrect. It appropriates the
title of a quite distinct treatise from the pen of
the Venerable Bede; and, further, misrepresents
the contents of the book. For this work with
which we have to deal is simply a commemoration sermon, relating the main particulars of the
life of Ceolfrid, the honoured personal friend of
Benedict Biscop, founder of the Monastery of
St. Peter and St. Paul, situate at Wearmouth
and Jarrow in the ancient kingdom of Northumbria. Ceolfrid long survived his friend and
proved himself to be, not only a helpful coadjutor, but also a worthy successor, to the first
and greatest abbot of this northern monastery.
The period of his life thereat coincides exactly
with that dealt with in the better known work

B

of Bede, the formal title of which is *The Life
of the Blessed Abbots Benedict, Ceolfrid, Eosterwini, Sigfrid, and Hwaetberht,* the other
book, with which we are concerned, describing
itself as *The Life of the Most Holy Ceolfrid,*
the original designation of each being precisely
true to the intention and drift of the two several
works. That confusion, however, should have
arisen between them is no great matter for wonder ; for they deal to a large extent with the
same place at the same period of history, and
much of the subject-matter is common to both.

Little surprise need be felt if Bede's volume
obtained from the first the greater notoriety.
Apart from its literary merits, of which more
will be said hereafter, it gives us by far the fuller
account of the founder of the monastery. The
personality of Benedict Biscop will always be
distinctly interesting ; he is the cultured man of
his day, a lover of books and of art and of all
things ecclesiastical. The work before us, however, does not profess to dwell on his many gifts
and opportunities ; they were hardly within its
scope. In another point again it labours at a
disadvantage. The anonymous author was in
no way the equal of Bede. He would not be
listened to, as was the great scholar whose fame
was already spreading beyond the limits of

Northumbria, and even of England. The marvel really is that this little book, composed at the same age and in the same monastery, has somehow contrived to survive. That it has done so is well; for had it perished we should have lost a very sweet story which all but certainly relates an incident in the life of Bede himself. And, moreover, we should have missed the portraiture of a character of singular goodness, if of secondary greatness, an example of life not too high for our own imitation.

It will not be deemed unfitting that this translation—the first published English version, as it is believed, of the Life of Ceolfrid—should make its appearance in the immediate vicinity of his own monastery of St. Peter. Editor and publishers have alike by birth or long residence an intimate acquaintance with the places where Ceolfrid spent his longest term of usefulness. At the outset of their work they desire to express very grateful thanks to those who have enabled them to complete it in the fullest possible manner; to the Reverend Chas. Plummer, fellow of Corpus Christi College, Oxford, and to the delegates of the Clarendon Press for much derived or quoted from Mr. Plummer's valuable edition of the historical works of Bede; to Mr. C. H. Turner and to the same publishers for per-

mission to make use of his account of the Green-
well leaf; and to the publishers of the *Church
Quarterly Review* for permission to reprint Mr.
Low's article on *The Codex Amiatinus.*

The duty falls upon those who thus bring forward into the present the story of the long distant past to lay before their readers the setting
of this ancient biography. The tale of Ceolfrid
will, we think, be the better understood, if some
account be first given of the conditions of contemporary Church life in Northumbria, the leading feature of which, as will at once be seen, is
the prevalence and influence of the monastic
bodies. The succeeding sections of this introduction will therefore attempt to deal with this
and other kindred subjects. Something will be
said of the age to which Ceolfrid belongs; of
his personal history and character as made
known or to be inferred from the records that
have been preserved to us; of the friendships
which he made, and of the homes in which he
dwelt at Wearmouth and at Jarrow; and last
of all the two existing accounts of him must be
considered, and especially that which is presented
in this volume, the text of which has its own
peculiar features and history, and contains at
least one passage which requires more than or-
dinary attention.

I.—NORTHUMBRIAN CHRISTIANITY IN THE DAYS OF CEOLFRID.

A.D. 642—716.

The dates which define the limits of our subject mark out a period of seventy-four years in the age of the Saxon Heptarchy. We find our country divided into at least seven kingdoms, of which we observe that two in the first instance specially invite attention. The conflict for supremacy lies between Pagan Mercia and Christian Northumbria. The invasion of the Mercian King Penda in the year 633 had appeared almost to have annihilated the northern kingdom. Then King Oswald comes forward to restore its fortunes, and in 634 completely routs the invaders at the battle of Heavenfield, five miles north of Hexham. He in his turn is defeated and slain in south-east Lancashire in the year which saw the birth of Ceolfrid. Thirteen years later (in 655) Penda himself falls at the battle of the river Winwaed, which is supposed to have taken place in the vicinity of Leeds. The political power of Mercia is now entirely broken, and Northumbria becomes the greatest of the English kingdoms. This position she maintains for a period of thirty years under her two great kings Oswy and Ecgfrid. The latter is slain in a conflict with the Picts at Nechtans-

mere in Dumfriesshire in the year 685. He is
succeeded by his half-brother Aldfrid, who for
twenty years reigns with credit over a territory
diminished to the north and west. The last
eleven years of Ceolfrid's life (705-716) corres-
pond with the reign of the boy king Osred,
under whom the political influence of the northern kingdom shows distinct signs of weakening.

The part of England, then, in which Ceolfrid's
life was spent was at that time of no mean reputation. In things secular it would have its
own great advantages. Under the rule of brave
and able men—for the most part decidedly good
men—all that was best would have its fair opportunities. Our great authority for the history
of this period is, of course, the Venerable Bede,
whose whole life appears to have been associated with Northumbria. Noted in his own day
for his great learning, he has been no less con-
spicuous in the settled judgement of after ages
for the wide outlook of his mind and his rare
love of truth. Bede was fortunately an eccle-
siastic of no narrow type ; he loves the English
people hardly less than he loves the Christian
faith. We are assured that we have from his
pen an accurate description of the events and
movements which were of greatest interest to
the thoughtful Englishmen of his day. The

matter of first moment was the establishment of the Christian religion, and in regard to this question Northumbria was quite prepared to take a leading part.

The object thus kept in view was truly great, and therefore all the more sure to awaken interest. It was calculated to enlist the sympathies of the heart as well of the mind. It became an end for which kings no less than priests laboured with the deep sincerity of convinced believers. There have been times in the history of every nation, when religion has been the popular topic of general thought, and when the strife of arms as much as that of tongues has been with the best men a contention for the truth. One such period in the history of England occurred in the days of Ceolfrid. The State, then in its primitive form of monarchy, united with the Church in the settlement of conditions which should be favourable to the permanence and extension of Christianity. This was for both the supreme business of the day. It was but natural that in their efforts they should rely on the strength of that great ecclesiastical force which was as truly powerful amongst the Celtic nationalities as in those countries which bowed to the Roman sway.

The men of the north and west were the parents of Northumbrian Christianity in so far as it had become a really popular movement. The religious views of kings and people had been strongly tinged with Scottish and Irish peculiarities. The various grades of holy orders were indeed held to have their special potency. Bishops occupied a high place amongst royal courts, and priests and deacons were honoured officials of the Church. But in the general estimation of men the position of the abbot as the head of a monastery was of leading importance. It will be well for us to realize this. Otherwise we might underrate the high place of the dignity to which Ceolfrid rose. The truth is that, apart from the glory that in time accrued to Wearmouth and Jarrow by the reputation of their great scholar Bede, that large and well ordered monastery was of itself a notable fact in the political and spiritual life of the Northumbrian kingdom. It represented religion established in ample force in the realm of King Ecgfrid; and to very many persons religion meant in those days what it still means to most of us, not the establishment of a stately hierarchy, not the crowd of numbers, or the splendour of fabrics, or the pomp of services, or the eloquence of sermons, but above all things the quiet and consistent holiness of devoted and saintly men. The pattern of this was exhibited specially by the monks, whose life in consequence came to be designated as the Religious Life.

To live this life was the first and best ideal of monasticism as practised originally in those distant regions of the East in which it found its birth, and brought from thence to the outlying parts of north-western Europe. The monasteries of Ireland and Scotland consisted of groups of isolated cells, gathered round some place of common worship, and enclosed by some rude rampart that marked the separation of each and all from the thoughtless world, which, as of old, was given over to its own passing concerns, and forgetful of Him to whom it owed, first its existence, and now also its redemption. In these communities every man's life was set apart by itself, as the one thing for which the individual was to be responsible ; each was to meditate and to pray and to watch in the presence of his God alone. This will account for the habit, frequent even amongst men who were or might have been supremely useful to their fellow men, of withdrawing themselves into a privacy of retirement which looks to us very much like a forsaking of opportunities. An instance of this will meet us in the case of Ceolfrid's own brother Cynefrid; another, much better known, is seen in that of the great St. Cuthbert, in regard to whom we cannot fail to observe that the hermit arrested the attention of the world as the bishop had never been able to do. We may say that in this case the world judged ill; but the fact remains that the highest value was set on the life that drew apart from men, and dedicated itself to God.

Of this sort of monasticism Ceolfrid must have known something during his four years' stay at Gilling. It was evidently the form of the religious life to which his brother became increasingly devoted. He would think of him after his departure to Ireland as now more than ever withdrawn from the world. It seems probable that the foundation of Gilling represented something by way of compromise between the views of the king and of the queen who had established it. The two brothers left it in different directions, and Ceolfrid sought a home in a monastery of a stricter character. This he found amongst the Benedictines of Ripon, a band of men gathered together by Wilfrid, the ardent champion in all things of the Roman fashion. Whatever we may think of the personal character of this great man—concerning which point his own disciple Bede is eloquently silent—we shall at least allow that he was as sincere in his beliefs, as he was successful in their propagation ; this much he testified by a life of much loss and self-sacrifice. The new form of monasticism with which Ceolfrid at this time came into closer touch, undoubtedly proved more permanent and more fruitful than that which preceded it. On this account alone we may well pause to observe its features ; all the more so, because it reached a very high degree of perfection in the monastery over which Ceolfrid was eventually called to preside.

The story of Benedict of Nursia, who must be carefully distinguished from his Northumbrian namesake, has been told many times over, and is easily accessible to all readers. It lies outside the scope of our present work. The case is otherwise in regard to his opinions and the principles on which he grounded the system of monasticism with which his name will be always connected. These appear to have been three in number. They mark him out as a reformer, not as a revolutionary. First he maintained the traditional ideas of silence and solitude, of reverence before God, and the cultivation of the individual soul. This was but to reaffirm a tenet theoretically at any rate received and approved. Next he asserted the grace of a lowly life, but gave it more honour and usefulness by making it a life of industrious service. But his special claim to future respect was that he made each of his monasteries a true and compact society, insisting much upon the mutual relations of the members of the brotherhood. Each of them had his several position to fill, higher, it might be, or lower. On the part of rulers he taught consideration, and obedience on the part of those that were ruled. The consideration, no doubt, largely vanished, when the abbot was a man rather of power than love, but the rigid obedience of the Benedictine monk secured to the ecclesiastical world both within and without the monasteries a sound system of order, which in its turn gave permanence and continuity to the institutions of the Church. The founder of this method had undoubtedly the genius of a statesman. He was far-sighted and he was practical. He prepared his followers each to know his place in the monastery, and to fulfil his appointed task, every one of them thus ministering to the welfare of the whole body. In such a community individual talents would in time find their proper scope, and the powers, physical, intellectual, and spiritual, would have their regular and alternative exercise. There was something in this method beyond the attractiveness of personal piety;

there was the promise of permanence and development. And yet Benedict valued highly the saintliness of the older monasticism, and taught it both by word and example. But this further he understood, that in the moral world no good thing lasts but by good government, and that good government is based upon discipline and order. It is hardly necessary to say that his conclusions were right; history itself has stamped them as true. The old-fashioned monasticism, whether of the East or of the West, in course of time passed away; that which was taught by Benedict lived and prevailed. We do indeed hear of new bodies of monks in later days; but in fact they ought not to be called so; they were simply reformations and revivals of the Benedictine models; the outcome of periods of neglect succeeded by the resuscitation of principles which had been tried and approved in this first great era of reform.

This then was the system which, during Ceolfrid's middle life was gradually supplanting that which had been introduced by those missionaries from Iona, by whose labours Christianity had been first endeared to the people of Northumbria. It had to fight its way to popular regard, and it was quite prepared to do so; for its adherents were a well disciplined force,

eager to assert the corporate as against the in-
dividualistic idea of the religious life, men who
believed most of all in order and obedience, and
whose practice was in strict accordance with
their beliefs. Amongst such persons, valuing
as they did the principle of command, it was an
easy matter to look upwards towards a supreme
head. It will not surprise us to find that their
efforts obtained the papal appreciation, and that
they themselves welcomed the papal benediction.
It was natural that those whose business it was to
present religion in visible and imposing form
should seek some living overlord. And the official
person who claimed ecclesiastical sovreignty re-
joiced in the possession of such willing subjects.
The gratification of both parties was mutual.
A letter of privilege, limiting in some way or
other the authority of the local bishop, was a
source of pride to the monastery; an aged abbot
is commended to the fatherly care of the pope,
who acknowledges in courteous terms his readi-
ness to receive him. We see already, and that
in no unattractive form, the connection which
eventually became so strong between the monks
in England and their superior at Rome.

The age of Ceolfrid is, for good or ill, a period
of change. An external ecclesiastical force is
making itself felt. In its desire to unify Christ-

ian usages it seems to affect disastrously the worthy spirit of patriotism. So keen is its attention to religious affairs that it remains quite unconscious of its own indifference to national interests. We notice this in the importance attached to what to us seem trifling matters. Our biographer's great contemporary, Bede, is apparently unconcerned at the failing fortunes of Northumbria : it is to him a much more serious matter that all persons do not observe the same Easter, and that all monks do not wear the same tonsure. The last named grievance may with us naturally raise a smile : to the Benedictine monk it was a gross scandal, which he set himself zealously to remove. His whole-hearted devotion to his order indicates the adoption of a line of thought and conduct which is to become momentous in ecclesiastical history. Henceforth if men love to dwell on the past, they will be directed to the stories of the martyrs, whose relics have come to them from foreign lands ; if they seek a change of scene, they will be urged to make a pilgrimage to Rome. Merry England will always love music, but the music of the Church will for many centuries come from abroad. The scholars of many generations will write and speak in Latin. So it comes to pass that the records of English history for the time become scanty. The historians are inmates of the cloister, and the life of the convent is self-absorbed. Its great events are grants or purchases of small estates. The death of an abbot is indeed worthy of note; but no details are given of the slaughter at Nechtansmere. And yet King Ecgfrid had at least deserved some remembrance from those to whom his charity had given a home. We should like to have heard that he was missed by the persons whom he had thus befriended.

We should like too, to have known more about the life of our forefathers, least and greatest; something of their homes and surroundings, of their times of war and peace, of their arts and crafts, of their cultivation of the soil, and their sailing on the sea; of their social life and intellectual condition; something about their occupations and recreations; something about the women and the children. A thousand matters of interest have been left untold. And yet, even if very much be lost to us, we ought to be thankful for what has been preserved. And indeed we have good cause for being so.

For it does so happen, that even in institutions, where all things are settled and ordered in one uniform routine, where all goes by cus-

tom and habit, and personal individuality appears to have next to no scope, there may be
found here and there a soul which cannot be
quite forced into the common mould; to whose
gifts and graces the timely occasion may allow
at least some play, and whose real worth may
win for itself first encouragement, and then
power. The monastery of St. Peter and St.
Paul was fortunate in this respect. Thanks to
its founder it was from its beginning a centre of
culture and learning : it had its countless supply
of books of all kinds ; the walls and ceilings of
its churches were bright with pictures. Here
was the apparatus, and here the environment,
that prepared at once for usefulness and for fame
the greatest scholar of his age. Here Bede
spent the long years of his life, writing in that
excellent Latin which none of his contemporaries knew how to equal, much less to excel.
Here he rightly interpreted the Scriptures by
comparing spiritual things with spiritual, the
old with the new, the type with the antitype,
after the fashion of the artists who adorned the
walls of his church at Jarrow ; setting forth
doctrine in allegory, that should display, and not
obscure, the truth. He worked it may be all
the better as being in the company of other
skilful workmen. For the monastery had its

c

art and its music, no less than its learning; and beside the scholars there were singers and painters and architects, and perhaps not least of all the copyists whose transcriptions of the Scripture have in one instance at least survived to our own day. In such a home as this there was no misapplication of means provided or of leisure secured. The treasures given for the wealth of these men had not as yet become an occasion of falling.

With the after history of the monastery at Wearmouth and Jarrow this volume has little to do. Not much is known about the matter. The reputation of the house appears to have remained respectable; its literary and educational traditions would help to keep it so. It never could have become the sort of place, which is described in Bede's very sad letter to Bishop Ecgbert, a habitation for those who meant to live only the idle or the selfish life. But on the other hand it was not likely that its abbots should be as great as their great founder, or as able administrators as his chosen coadjutor and successor. If they were more than average men, they have been unfortunate in lacking their chronicler. As it is the very record of their names is imperfect. The dead past has here indeed buried its dead, and we turn our thoughts towards the good man whose name and fame have survived to us, and of whom it is our business in this place to speak.

II.—THE LIFE AND CHARACTER OF CEOLFRID.

The work which is the subject of this publication supplies us with nearly all the known details of the personal life of Ceolfrid. Our only other available authority is the Venerable Bede. Anything further which he tells us we trust we shall not fail to notice, but before doing so it will not be amiss for us to state in chronological order the leading incidents of his career, and also such events in local, political, and ecclesiastical history as affected seriously the Northumbrian kingdom and Church, or may have determined more or less his own views and conduct. These are as follows :—

A.D. 642. Birth of Ceolfrid. This year Oswald, King of the Northumbrians, is slain in battle with the pagan Mercians, and is succeeded by his brother Oswy.

644. Oswin makes himself king in Deira (Yorkshire), a man of great piety, and a friend of monks.

648. Wilfrid begins his career as a monk at Lindisfarne.

651. Oswin murdered at the instigation of Oswy, who at the desire of his queen and in expiation of

his crime founds a monastery at Gilling. Aidan, first Celtic Bishop of the Northumbrians, dies, and is succeeded by Finan, a monk from Iona.

655. Battle of the Winwaed. Penda, king of the Mercians is slain. Victory of Oswy. Fall of Paganism, and triumph of Christianity. Highest period of Northumbrian power commences.

657. Hilda founds the Abbey of Whitby.

660. Ceolfrid enters the monastery at Gilling.

661. Bishop Finan dies and is succeeded by Colman, a monk from Iona.

664. Synod of Whitby : the Easter controversy discussed. King Oswy, convinced by the arguments of Wilfrid, abandons the Celtic usage, and adopts that of the Roman party. Ceolfrid leaves Gilling, and at the invitation of Wilfrid enters his monastery at Ripon. Bishop Colman retires to Iona. Tuda Bishop of Lindisfarne.

669. Ceolfrid ordained priest by Wilfrid at Hexham.

669-70. Ceolfrid visits the monasteries in Kent and East Anglia.

671. Death of King Oswy. Accession of his son Ecgfrid.

673. Biscop, having obtained land for the purpose of founding a monastery at Wearmouth, asks Wilfrid to allow Ceolfrid to come to him, and obtains his request. Birth of Bede in the territory of the monastery.

674. The monks' quarters at Wearmouth erected.

675. Biscop goes to Gaul for masons to build his church. Revolt of the nobler monks against Ceolfrid's strictness. He retires to Ripon, and is recalled by Biscop on his return.

678-80. Ceolfrid accompanies Biscop to Rome. They bring back with them John the chanter.

680. Bede is placed by his relatives under Biscop's charge.

681. See of Hexham founded. Tunbert bishop. King Ecgfrith grants to Biscop a further estate at Jarrow. The new foundation there, consisting of twenty-two persons, is committed to the care of Ceolfrid with the title of abbot. Bede at the desire of his relatives accompanies Ceolfrid. First church at Jarrow (chancel of the present church) built.

684. The great church at Jarrow commenced.

685. Dedication of the same. King Ecgfrid is slain in battle at Nechtansmere (Dumfriesshire), and is succeeded by his half-brother Aldfrid. Commencement of the decline of Northumbria.

686. Plague at Jarrow. Only Ceolfrid and Bede left to conduct the services. First visit of Adamnan, abbot of Iona, to the monastery of St. Peter and St. Paul.

688. Second visit of Adamnan. John bishop of Hexham. Ceolfrid constituted abbot of the whole monastery.

689. Death of Biscop.

692. Bede receives deacon's orders from Bishop John at the bidding of Ceolfrid.

703. Bede is ordained priest by Bishop John at Ceolfrid's bidding.

705. Death of King Aldfrid, who is succeeded by his son Osred.

706. Wilfrid bishop of Hexham.

710. Acca, bishop of Hexham. Naiton, king of the Picts, sends to Ceolfrid for architects, and advice as to the Easter and tonsure controversies.

716. The Scots at Ionà adopt the Roman Easter. Resignation and death of Ceolfrid. Death of King Osred.

It will be observed that the details of the above chronological table are confined to events connected with the history of Northumbria. But even so we have enough to tell us that Ceolfrid lived in stirring times. Throughout his life he must have been acquainted with the leading personages, both in Church and State, who figured in the life of the northern kingdom. We can hardly doubt that the two good kings, Ecgfrid and Aldfrid, must have paid occasional visits to the monastery which they had founded and endowed. The abbot himself would be respected by them as being the son of one of King Oswy's thanes ; and, though he might not be so frequently at court as his predecessor seems to have been, yet his high station and indisputable merits would ensure for him, when he came there, a very courteous welcome. The bishops of Hexham seem to have been on good terms with the monastery of St. Peter and St. Paul. Jealousy between bishops and monks, so notorious in later days, was in these earlier times a thing unknown.

Our biography, as above stated, omits much that we should have wished to hear, and we must take for granted the existence of acquaintanceships and friendships, where there is good reason to think that we may safely do so. But the picture of Ceolfrid's life would be hardly complete without something more than a passing notice of some of those persons with whom we know him to have been brought into close contact, the men who helped to form his habits and opinions, and were closely bound to him by common interests and familiarity of life.

First among these was his own brother Cynefrid, through whose influence in all probability Ceolfrid himself became a monk. Of the beautiful end of his short career the work before us has something to say. He died a comparatively young man in Ireland, whither he had gone to find a quiet retreat for the study of the Scriptures. He was succeeded in the abbacy of Gilling by his own cousin and Ceolfrid's, Tunbert, who was destined seventeen years later to be the first bishop of Hexham. The new abbot appears to have shared the views of Ceolfrid at the period of transition, when both together left their first monastery under the influence and at the request of a not very distant neighbour, who had founded and governed the rising monastery of Ripon. This person is known to all readers of history by the name of St. Wilfrid.

Into the details of the long and extraordinary
career of this great man it is not here our pro-
vince to enter. They may be read elsewhere
in many volumes, which all alike represent to
us a person of great activity and resolution, an
originator, a disputant, a ruler, a missionary,
often giving offence and suffering for it, driven
by his opponents and much more by his own wil-
ful spirit into many lands ; always on the move,
and always finding something to do ; changing
his home repeatedly, but unchanging in mind
and purpose. The one principle above all others
that actuated his life was that of the promotion
of the unity of the Church on earth under the
primacy of the Bishop of Rome, as being the
successor, as he believed, of the Apostle St.
Peter. Holding these views, he naturally became a partisan of Roman as opposed to Celtic
forms and usages. Gilling was probably in some
measure open to Celtic influences ; Ripon was
purely Benedictine. The removal of Tunbert
and Ceolfrid from the one place to the other
shows that they were prepared to lay aside the
traditions of St. Aidan and to adopt the views
of St. Wilfrid.

This event took place in the year 664. The
date is significant It is the year of the settlement of the Easter controversy. Those who

wish to master the history of this long-debated
and peculiar subject may be safely referred to
Dr. Stokes's *Ireland and the Celtic Church,*
(ch. viii.), and to the excursus in Mr. Plummer's *Bede, (vol. II., p. 348)*. Bede's own
views on the question may be found in his treatise on the Reckoning of Times, and also in that
more accessible work, the *Ecclesiastical History, (bk. V., ch. 21)*. He enters into the
matter with much zest, as befits a scholar who
is exceedingly fond of figures and computations.
The nature of the controversy was as follows :
—Both parties were agreed that the Easter festival should be celebrated in the first month, in
the third week, and on the Lord's day. The
first month was defined to be that whose moon
reached her complement (or fulness) either on
the day of the vernal equinox, or next after it.
The Celts, misunderstanding the Scriptural
rule as to the date of the paschal observance,
held that the third week of the month began
on the fourteenth and ended on the twentieth
day of the lunar month ; with the Roman party
the computation was from the fifteenth to the
twenty-first day. Hence from time to time it
happened that the Celts observed their feast a
week earlier than the Romans. To Wilfrid and
his friends this was a serious matter. How could

the Church be one in heart and mind, if its members could not agree to unite in the celebration of the Lord's Resurrection?

With Bede truth was always a consideration of first moment, and that in every way; hence no doubt his love for mathematical accuracy. But most men were too little expert to share his calculations. Such persons were guided by considerations of a different sort. Our readers will probably know that the prevailing argument with King Oswy was that the Roman practice was that of St. Peter, that St. Peter held the keys of heaven, and that it would be best to make terms with him. This was the logic of Wilfrid, and Oswy found it convincing. He decided that his people should henceforth follow the Roman style in the observance of the festival of Easter.

It is quite probable that others beside King Oswy saw good reason to change their views as a result of the synod of Whitby. We may well believe that this was the case with Ceolfrid himself. We are told that in this year he was invited by Wilfrid to join him at Ripon, that he accepted the invitation and subjected himself to the life of rule—an expression which no doubt means the strict discipline of the Benedictine

order,—obviously before this date only partially
known to him. He was there probably admit-
ted to the diaconate, and, as we know, within
five years of the great synod, to the priesthood.
It is clear that Wilfrid had marked him down as
a useful man. On his elevation to the last-
named office he takes a journey with a view of
learning to the full the several duties of a monk
and of a priest. He does not go northward to
Iona, but rather to the monasteries of eastern
and southern England : for his object is to acquaint himself as perfectly as possible with all
that could be taught by men who had been
trained after the Roman type. We observe that
throughout his career he aimed at thoroughness
of knowledge and correctness of action in the
performance of his work both as monk and
priest ; and that, not after the tradition of his
fathers, but after the manner of the teaching of
Wilfrid.

The excellence to which he attained in the
course of his studies at this period of his life
commended him to the notice of a new friend.
About three or four years after Ceolfrid's ordination to the priesthood, the English Benedict
(whom by way of distinction we shall hereafter
call by his other name of Biscop) was prepar-
ing to found his monastery on the Wear. He

required the services of some monk of accomplished orthodoxy, and competent also as a priest to minister at the altar. This latter qualification tells us implicitly that Biscop himself was not in priest's orders, and the tenor of his life as described to us in the two contemporary biographies appears to make it probable that the founder of the new establishment was all his days a layman. He was often, we are told, at the king's court, often also abroad; a man whose mind was comparatively free to indulge those artistic and æsthetic tastes, which contributed so effectually to the adornment of his monastery.

Biscop asked Wilfrid to spare him the services of Ceolfrid, and we learn that his request was granted. The two men became fellow workers and close friends; and the intimacy which thus began determined eventually the whole course of Ceolfrid's life. It was a real friendship, valued most of all, as it appears, by the greater man of the two. Ceolfrid could do without Biscop, but Biscop could not part with Ceolfrid. On no account would he repent of his choice. The predilection which he showed for his new acquaintance was at first resented by the highborn monks of Biscop's foundation. These of course would lead the others, and, on their abbot's first occasion of absence from home, they made things disagreeable for the new prior. Ceolfrid, for the sake of his own peace at once withdrew to Ripon. This was in the year 675. But on this occasion Biscop had not gone far; he soon returned home, and forthwith sought out Ceolfrid, and brought him back to the new monastery. When he next goes abroad he is careful to take his friend with him. They are absent for two years (678-80), and when they come home they bring with them John the chanter, by whose help the musical services of the monastery attain singular perfection and fame. We wonder whether it was Ceolfrid himself that secured the services of this person. No one, we are sure, would rejoice more than he in the advent of so distinguished and useful a visitor.

By this time, no doubt, all enmities have died down. Every one is prepared now to believe in Ceolfrid. When the new house at Jarrow is to be founded, the whole matter is entrusted to his care. The cultured Biscop leaves all to the practical Ceolfrid, and sets forth on yet another journey, from which he will return in time with pictures and books for the adornment of his churches and the instruction of their worshippers. And the day will come when he will

commit both houses, Wearmouth and Jarrow,
to the care of this one man. Our story will
assure us that he made no mistake in doing so.

Such then was the friendship of Biscop and
Ceolfrid, two men much unlike each other. We
shall probably be right, if we say, that, if the
better known character is the most interesting,
the personal worthiness of his friend did not
fall below his own.

The death of Biscop took place on January
12th, 689. The loss to Ceolfrid was no doubt
great. But it must have been at least in some
degree relieved, as he watched the progress
of the young scholar who was destined some
day to be the glory of his monastery. Bede,
now a lad of seventeen, had for eight years at
least been closely associated with him. We
gather this from a passage at the close of the
Ecclesiastical History, (bk. V., ch. 24), where
Bede says of himself :—" Born on the estate of
the same monastery, when I was seven years
old I was given by the care of my relatives to
the most reverend abbot Benedict, and afterwards to Ceolfrid, to be educated by them."

Two affirmations are, we think, here made :
first that Bede was a native of Wearmouth,

Biscop having returned to Northumbria in the year that Cenwealh king of Wessex died, i.e., in 672, and being probably in possession of his new estate early in the following year ; and next, which is to us at the moment of more interest, that the relatives of Bede placed him first in Benedict's charge, then in that of Ceolfrid. The meaning of this last statement will be at once perceived, when we recall the fact that in the year 682 certain monks and lay-brethren set forth from Wearmouth under the leadership of Ceolfrid to occupy the new buildings at Jarrow. Almost simultaneously Biscop left home for the Continent leaving Eosterwini to govern the older establishment. The relatives of Bede evidently preferred to entrust him to Ceolfrid, and their wish was gratified. Here then is another evidence of the confidence everywhere reposed in Ceolfrid.

We may well believe then that after this date Jarrow, as tradition has always held, became Bede's usual home. This he himself does not precisely state, mindful, no doubt, of the injunction of their great founder that the two houses should always be accounted as one. Unless any distinction is specially required Bede always speaks of "our monastery." But there can be no reason to suppose that the little lad who

helped Ceolfrid to chant the services at Jarrow
during the plague of 686 *(ch. 14)*, was any other
person than Bede himself, described as he further is by the preacher of our homily as a priest
still in the same monastery, and as a ready
recorder of Ceolfrid's praiseworthy deeds. It is
quite after the manner of Bede to omit this
anecdote from his *Lives of the Abbots;* he had
learnt well the lesson of humility, and it was not
his habit to talk about himself. If then we take
it that the tale speaks of Bede, we find in it a
proof that Bede made Jarrow his home. He
would be much no doubt at the greater monastery, but the quieter house may have been more
adapted for study, and a tradition long maintained and never disputed asserts that Jarrow
was the place of his death.

Bede then, as we may reasonably infer, was
generally to be found at the home whither he
had accompanied his friend and instructor. The
tuition of such a pupil must have been a great
delight to any teacher worthy of the name. The
master would rejoice in the swift progress of the
scholar, and the scholar would regard with grow-
ing affection the person of his friend and master.
We can think of Ceolfrid marvelling, as he must
often have done, at the attainments of this pro-
mising student, at his knowledge of Greek as

well as of Latin, of the classical as well as the sacred authors, at his original compositions in prose and verse, his treatises on chronology and history, geography, orthography and prosody, at his correspondence with bishops and scholars in the far distant south. He would be at once proud and thankful in regard to his great pupil. He would be glad to know that he could count on his help, when difficult questions were submitted to him. That he did so consult him is evident, as we think, in the case of the letter to Naiton *(Eccl. Hist., V. 21)*, the story of which seems to be here worthy of narration.

Towards the close of Ceolfrid's long reign, in the year 710, there came to the monastery of St. Peter and St. Paul a deputation from Naiton, king of the Picts, to discuss the Easter question of which we have already heard so much. The Celts of Scotland and Ireland had not hitherto acquiesced in the decision of the synod of Whitby. They were now, it is clear, beginning to feel their isolation, and to doubt whether they had been altogether wise in maintaining their own local usages. So King Naiton sends messages to Ceolfrid, probably well aware of the literary repute of his monastery, and asks him to state plainly the case of the orthodox party

D

in England, both in regard to the Easter controversy and to that other vexed subject, the tonsure of monks. The first matter needed very careful explanation, and this is given in the letter which Ceolfrid returns to Scotland. The arguments used are so clearly set forth as to denote the hand of one whose mastery of the subject was probably unequalled. We should have guessed them to be the work of Bede in any case ; they are in fact almost quoted from his volume on the *Reckoning of Times*. Things are different. however, when the question of the tonsure is reached. Are the Celts right in shaving the hair above the forehead, or the monks of other races, who shave the crown of the head? The writer of the reply sent to the king begins at this point to speak of a personal reminiscence; how he had long ago told a visitor from the north, Adamnan, abbot of Iona, that the tonsure now used in England was that of St. Peter, the other, the Scottish use, that of Simon Magus. Here we feel that we have Bede no longer with us. It is Ceolfrid who is speaking now, and he is using the logic of Wilfrid. On the more important and difficult question he had wisely consulted Bede.

How warmly the younger man returned the affection of his old friend is happily actually known to us. When the aged abbot of St. Peter and St. Paul revealed his determination to bid farewell to his monastery, and to end his days near the traditional scene of their martyrdom, the announcement was the cause of universal distress. Bede seems to have been for the time prostrated. A close intimacy subsisted between himself and Acca, the bishop of Hexham, to whom he dedicates many of his books. When he reaches the fourth volume of the *Commentary on Samuel* he apologises to the bishop for its tardy dispatch, due, as he says, to his own sudden anguish of mind at the departure of his late most reverend abbot. The event had indeed caused consternation in the monastery, and paralysed for the time the great powers of a very sane and cheerful man.

The resolution of Ceolfrid was probably somewhat suddenly adopted. A single word in the prefatory verses of the *Codex Amiatinus*—of which more will be said hereafter—plainly shows that he had not originally intended to resign his charge. What he had meant to do was to send that valuable copy of the Scriptures as a present to the Pope. This is distinctly stated in the dedicatory lines penned before the book left the monastery. He changed his mind and took it with him. We think that there was a reason for this, and that we have some light thrown upon the matter.

We have heard of King Naiton's interest in the Paschal question, and of the letter sent by Ceolfrid in answer to his enquiries. And we are told by Bede, that, on the receipt of that letter, he sought to enforce throughout his dominions the orthodox observance of Easter. But in spite of his efforts one church still continued to maintain the Celtic usage—the mother church of Iona, whose missionaries had converted Northumbria. In the year 715 there came to that monastery a devoted servant of God, Ecgberht by name; an Englishman, and probably a Northumbrian, who had spent much of his life in Ireland, where he seems to have been consecrated a bishop. He had resolved at one time to be a missionary to the Germans, but was bidden in a vision to go and teach the monasteries of Columba. He came accordingly to Iona, where he was very kindly received; and without much difficulty induced the monks to conform to the now general customs of the Church. At Easter, in the year 716, they celebrated the festival on the same day with the other churches of Britain. By this submission a long and weary dispute at last came to an end. May we not suppose that Ceolfrid heard of it and was glad? Now at last the heart of the mother was turned to the children, and that of the children would be turned to the mother. A day of peace and blessing was at hand. Ceolfrid had now nothing further for which to wait and to pray. The servant of the Lord might say his *Nunc Dimittis,* and enter into his rest.

The incidents of Ceolfrid's history present to us a character which naturally engages respect. It is beyond question that he was reckoned a true man, a strength and support to those about him. He was thorough and whole-hearted in his beliefs, and in the discharge of work; and he was very devoted and conscientious. Some doubt may perhaps arise as to whether he was an affectionate man. That he was so is not directly stated either in Bede's work or in that of the anonymous author. In regard to this point we must not fail to remember that both of these writers, as well as this particular subject of their memoirs, were inmates of a monastery. The tendency of monasticism is at least to keep the natural affections under control; in the case of devotees almost to abolish them.

Ceolfrid was a very strict disciplinarian—to himself as much as to others. Our story will tell us that when he left Wearmouth he observed of his fraternity, "never have I known such obedient men." This was his commendation of his household. Submission to rule had clearly become with him more than a principle; it was a test of high character. In the case of a person who held such views, it would not be surprising if the active powers of affection were somewhat dulled. He could hardly have been as loveable as St. Aidan, or as Bede's dear friend Acca, the bishop of Hexham. But still he must have been a man of warm and considerate feelings. We hear of his fervour in the correction of the unworthy; a good man who can be indignant is usually generous in his commendations. We read of his gentleness in the comforting of the weak; here was a wise and tender kindness. We are told that he was on fire with the love of God; that could be said of no cold heart. The affections of Ceolfrid, if guarded and governed, were none the less real; they were not so much mortified from the world as fostered for the highest ends. The knowledge of this, it may have been, drew closer the hearts of those who had to part with him; they grieved over his departure because he was good, and because they really loved him.

As to his intellectual and moral powers, he is credited by his contemporaries with a natural and practical shrewdness, with a staid gravity, an unfailing industry, and a studied faithfulness in the performance of his duties. He had high ideals and always aimed at the best. We are not surprised to find that with a mind so well ordered he excelled in the correctness of his music. His habit was to be frugal towards himself, and munificent to others. He would much rather give than take, and this it was that made him extremely sensitive of being under any obligation to friend or neighbour. This rather curious characteristic may still be frequently observed among the Northumbrians of the present day.

Of originality in any way he shows no trace, and the whole tenor of his life was such as to obscure this merit, if indeed, he ever possessed it. His business was to carry out what others designed, and to do so extremely well. Such men are valuable indeed; far more so than the small geniuses, who so gaily uproot and pull down, and then, if they can, set to work to build and to replant. The principles of the great Benedict were enough for Ceolfrid; to rule with charity and to obey with reverence. To strengthen the work of his friend Biscop, and that

without new developments of his own; to do
this so thoroughly and zealously as to make the
institutions which he ruled more than ever attractive and popular; to double the great library,
and to augment the membership of the brotherhood—these were the ambitions of Ceolfrid, the
successes which he desired and achieved.

III.—THE MONASTERY OF ST. PETER AND ST. PAUL AT WEARMOUTH AND JARROW.

Some attempt has now been made to help the
reader to realize the age and the society to which
the subject of our work belonged, and also to
fill up the circumstances of his life and the details of his history in so far as other existing
records allow. Our task will not, however, be
complete without some account of such literary
and material remains of the period, as are connected with our subject, and have been spared
to the present day. The anonymous Biography
will speak for itself. The similar work of Bede
will be compared and contrasted with it. The
story of the great Latin Bible—the famous
Codex Amiatinus, now in the Mediceo-Laurentian Library at Florence, has been once and
for all well told by the pen of the late Reverend
J. L. Low; and a reprint of his article appears

as an appendix to this book. Of a fragment of one of the sister pandects an illustration is given with this volume, and some notice of it and of other recovered pages of the same book will be found in their fit place at the close of his essay on the volume just mentioned. These are all alike precious relics of the past that declare the characters and the attainments of the men of the old Northumbrian monastery.

But this is not all that remains to us. We have no need to identify the places where Ceolfrid spent his life. Parts of the very churches where he worshipped, and of which indeed he assisted in the building, have fortunately been preserved to us. For the earliest existing portion of the church at Jarrow Ceolfrid was probably himself personally responsible ; in the erection of the still older church at Monkwearmouth the inseparable companion and fellow-helper of Biscop may be presumed to have had no inconsiderable share. Those who dwell near these buildings, and those, too, who at a greater or less distance shall peruse this volume, may alike be pleased to have some account of what is still left of the ancient monastery of St. Peter and St. Paul.

Of the conventual buildings of the seventh

century, apart from the churches, nothing now remains. We cannot definitely say whether the domestic quarters of the early monks lay to south or north or west. The tradition at Monk-wearmouth is that the old monastery stretched westward from the church of St. Peter, but the original entrance into the chamber over the former western porch (now the base of the tower) looks to the north, and there is a small closed doorway in the oldest part of Jarrow Church set in the same direction. The question must perhaps be left undecided. Our records tell us that at Monkwearmouth there were dining rooms and kitchens, and a dormitory for the monks with an oratory dedicated to St. Laurence attached to it. We know that the cemetery at the same place lay to the south-east of St. Peter's Church. A mediæval document referring to the "old church" as a granary implies to those who know the locality, that the then long disused church of St. Mary lay in a spot which may be supposed to be south-west of the same building. Of St. Peter's Church itself, however, a good deal more may be said.

This church, as it appeared as late as the be-ginning of the nineteenth century, lay on the ridge of a hill sloping gently to north and south,

the river Wear flowing along its southern side.
Its original west wall remains almost intact, with
a porch of the same period to the west of it,
having openings or doorways on its four sides.
Above it was a parvise or chamber (already mentioned) which was surmounted by a saddle roof,
in the western gable of which certain large and
now mutilated stones appear to have been carved
into a representation of the crucifixion. The
church itself, in spite of rebuildings, retains its
original height, the long, narrow and lofty nave
(roughly speaking, 60 × 20 × 30 feet) still pre-
serving its first dimensions, the proportions being
those of Solomon's Temple reduced every way
by one-third. The meaning of the above measurements is dwelt upon by Bede in one of his sermons ; they represent the length of faith, the
height of hope, and the breadth of charity.
The sanctuary has quite disappeared, removed
no doubt in mediæval times. Another example
in the county (that at Escomb) leads us to
infer that it was in the form of a cube, measuring 20 feet every way.

The settlement of monks at Jarrow took place
eight years after that at Monkwearmouth. The
party detached for the purpose consisted of 22 (or
at the least 17) persons under the superintend-

ence of Ceolfrid. Our writer will tell us that
all necessary buildings were erected before their
arrival ; one such would be a place for worship,
and this, we believe, is now the chancel of Jarrow
Church. Three years later, (the number of the
monks probably increasing), there arose to the
west of the older fabric, and separated some 13
feet from it, the church of St. Paul, which appears to have been precisely similar to that of
St. Peter. This we gather from pictures and
measurements which have been preserved from
the eighteenth century. This church was in later
times, by alterations which included the building
of the present tower, incorporated with the older
fabric. It was destroyed in the year 1783. The
Jarrow churches stood, and what remains of
them stands, on an eminence above the little
river Don at its confluence with the Tyne.

Flanking the old nave of Jarrow, as it was
in its last days, there were traces or portions of
a number of square apartments opening by semi-
circular arches into the church. This was no
doubt also the arrangement at Monkwearmouth.
These were the porches mentioned by Bede ;
they provided the monks, as we think, with
rooms for study and prayer, and the teaching
of scholars. This appears to be the reason

why rooms for such uses are not otherwise mentioned in the two contemporary records.

Such in brief outline appears to have been the construction of the churches of the twin monasteries. A full presentation of the evidence for some statements here alleged is beyond the compass of the present volume.* But what has been above noted with reference to the buildings of the age of Ceolfrid will have its use for those who are fortunate enough to be able to visit the scenes of his far distant life. They will think of him not only as he was, but where he was, and the story of his career will, we hope, become to them all the more real.

IV.—THE BIOGRAPHIES.

The attention of our readers must now be turned to the two books which profess to give us the history of the Abbot Ceolfrid. One, by far the better known of the two, is of course the work of the celebrated Bede. The other is the anonymous Life of which our translation immediately follows. If our surmise is correct,

---

* A more detailed description of the alterations at Jarrow as above suggested in the Monkwearmouth and Jarrow section of *Memorials of Old Durham*, (Geo. Allen & Co.) For the measurements see Boyle's *Guide to the County of Durham*, pp. 581-589.

that the priest mentioned in chapter 14 is Bede
himself, this book, it will be observed, speaks of
him as still living. Bede died on Ascension
Day, in the year 735. Our work therefore, like
his own, must have been composed between the
midsummer of 716 and the date last mentioned.
We should say that it belongs rather to the close
than the commencement of this period. Speaking of the monks who returned from the burial
place of Ceolfrid, the writer adopts the imperfect
tense : " they used to tell us " so and so. Those
who did so had evidently all passed away.

As to the personality of the author of the
anonymous Life, something may be inferred from
the work which he has left behind him. He
was probably a younger man than Bede. One
event above all others is that which he specially
remembers—Ceolfrid's farewell to his monastery ; every detail connected with it is vividly
impressed upon his mind, and his narrative is
all the more touching from its simple description
of this memorable occurrence. The difference
is quite marked between his account of this and
the other incidents which he relates. As to his
general character and ability something may be
learned by a comparison of his work with Bede's
Lives of the Abbots.

Of the two books we observe that each is the production of a monk, and confines itself to the history of a monastery and its inmates. The two writers are true Benedictines, with much reverence for the principle of submission to authority, and a high respect for the See of Rome. Each rejoices in the privilege which his house enjoys, and in the state of independence which it has thereby secured. Each reminds us of the routine of the daily services, and of the constant practice of the recitation of the Psalter. Each is singularly indifferent to national events and the doings of the world outside of the cloister. Each by saying little or nothing about long years in succession bears witness to the regularity and monotony of his daily life, and the subdued calm of a peaceful and well ordered monastery.

On the other hand, as we read over the two stories we are aware of differences. We notice first that the two books have their distinct subjects; one is the history of a monastery, the other that of an abbot. The greater writer deals with the larger subject, and this is as it should be. For Bede is the master of a really literary style; his vocabulary is abundant, and his periods are rich and full. There is a wider view before him, and we feel that he is somehow cognizant of a rather larger world. To him kings and bishops are something more than bare names; he has some respect or even admiration for some of those in high estate. He has a much greater interest in things beautiful than his nameless contemporary, and describes somewhat minutely the pictures which adorned the churches of Monkwearmouth and Jarrow. It is he who tells how glass was brought to England, of the uses made of it, and of the introduction amongst us of a new art. Of course he makes reference to books, which are to him something more than so many items in a library; and twice over he puzzles us by quotations from poems which he knew and we do not know. He brightens his own work with illustrations, and in his description of the Abbot Eosterwini sketches out for us the features of a very attractive personality. The anonymous author is on the other hand a plainer man, whose first business is to stick to his subject, and to relate particulars in due order. He was evidently not quite within the inner circle of those who read the deeper feelings of men in authority, and it is quite probable that the abbot whom he reverenced was, as a rule, a man of reserve. He would not therefore apprehend so thoroughly

the secret struggle of a conscientious soul. He
would not have understood such a man as Biscop, but he could appreciate the steady regularity of the plain and practical Ceolfrid. He
is a very fair scholar, and his Latin is simple
and good, though not fluent; if his language
represents the usual style of the average monk
on the Wear or the Tyne, it speaks well both
for teachers and learners. Probably the whole
monastery benefited by the presence of its greatest scholar, pre-eminent as he was above all
writers and theologians in the two centuries to
which his life belongs.

The historian, and such a historian as Bede,
was sure to attract the interest of the world to
a degree beyond that which was likely to be
reached by the lowlier biographer and homilist.
Hence we need not be surprised to hear that
only two manuscripts have been found which
contain the Life of Ceolfrid. The older of
these, the Harleian manuscript of the tenth
century, is believed to be the parent of the
Digby manuscript two centuries later in date.
The more recent manuscript supplies from time
to time sensible corrections : on the other hand
it is marred by interpolations from the contemporary work of Bede.

E

The Latin text of the Harleian copy was first printed by Stevenson in 1841, and reprinted by Giles in 1843. The Digby manuscript was first collated by Mr. Plummer for his edition of Bede's Historical Works, 1896.

It is much to be wished that the later copyist, who is fond of making improvements, had exercised his skill on a large and corrupt passage towards the close of the work. We shall hear that, on Ceolfrid's departure from Wearmouth, his successor Hwaetbercht wrote a letter commending him to the kindness of Pope Gregory II. A very beautiful letter it is in spite of its long and involved sentences. The answer sent in reply is given by the author of our work, who tells us that it bears witness as to the Pope's opinion of the aged abbot. This is no doubt the case, but we wish that that witness had been more clearly expressed. The letter, as we have it, consists of one long and cumbrous paragraph, originally extremely clumsy in its composition, and now defaced by numerous blunders. Something, however, may be made of it; there are glimmerings of light through the darkness, and we discern the gist of what the writer meant to say. The words do not lack dignity, humility, courteousness and goodwill. But still there remains the problem—how did the text get into such confusion ?

The answer to this question may some day be given by some one acquainted with documents of the same age and from the same place. Such an one may in time unravel the errors which abound in the passage as we have it. The letter cannot be considered a forgery ; a forger is a copyist of things that exist, and this document represents no sort of style that ever was. Was the handwriting of its scribe peculiar and so misread by English readers? It may be that Bede knew our writer's book : if so, or in any case, why does he not give us his version of this letter? Was it because he saw in it the work of some careless secretary, who had been entrusted with the copying of what he could not understand, and had done his task so badly that the less said about it the better? Our author at any rate is free from all critical scruples. Here was a letter from Rome : for the glory of the monastery its contents should be recorded.

And now our readers must be left to hear the anonymous preacher tell the story of the good old abbot whose rule was, as he conceived, nearly perfect. It is going on for twenty years since

his death : many of the survivors of that event
have passed away. Before he, too, shall join
them he will try to save from oblivion the memory of a wise and useful man. He will tell
the tale of Ceolfrid, and write it down, that, if
God so will, posterity may know it and the
children that are yet unborn.

THE

Life of Ceolfrid

A

COMMEMORATION SERMON

DELIVERED IN THE

MONASTERY OF ST. PETER AND ST. PAUL

AT

WEARMOUTH AND JARROW

IN OR ABOUT

THE YEAR OF OUR LORD'S INCARNATION

DCCXXXIII.

Hebrews xiii., 7.

*Here beginneth the Life of the most holy
Ceolfrid, abbot, under whom the blessed
Beda assumed the garb of holy religion,
and after whose death according to his
merits he won[1] the palm of eternal felicity.*

1. The Apostle Paul in his epistle to the
Hebrews thus teacheth : "Remember them that
had the rule over you, who spake to you the
word of God, whose faith follow considering the
outgoing of the life they lived."[2]   Whence
it is clearly evident, dearly beloved, that ye do
exceedingly well, in that ye command that dis-
course be made in commemoration of that most
reverend father, and our own ruler, Ceolfrid,
who spake unto us the word of God.   For in
very deed he was such, that not only the outgoing of his consecrated life, but also its incom-
ing and its progress should be duly traced ; and
that the constancy of his unfeigned faith should
be a pattern for us to follow.

2. For, being the child of noble and god-
fearing parents, and himself from the first years
of his boyhood devoted to the pursuit of the
virtues, when he was all but entering on his

eighteenth year, laying aside the garb of this
world he chose rather to become a monk, and
entered the monastery, which, being situate in
the place that is called Gilling, had been under
the rule of his brother Cynefrid, a religious man
and loveable in the sight of God, but had lately
been committed by him to the care of their
common kinsman, Tunbert (who afterwards was
consecrated prelate of the church of Hexham),
Cynefrid himself withdrawing to Ireland[3] in
his zeal for the study of the scriptures, and as
being desirous withal of serving the Lord with
less hindrance in tears and prayers.

3. And so, being devoutly welcomed by his
aforesaid kinsman, Ceolfrid himself behaved
with the greater devotion, giving his mind continually to reading, to labour, and to monastic
discipline. And not long after this a pestilence
spread far and wide, and the said Cynefrid
and other Englishmen of noble birth, who with
a view to the studying of the scriptures had
preceded him to Ireland, passed from fleeting
death unto abiding life ; and Tunbert and with
him Ceolfrid and a good many brothers of
the monastery of Gilling at the invitation of
Bishop Wilfrid withdrew to the monastery of
Ripon, where Ceolfrid submitting himself ac-

cording to the manner to the life of discipline
was in the course of time chosen and ordained to
the priesthood by the above named bishop, being then about twenty-seven years of age. Soon
after his ordination, being desirous to acquaint
himself to the utmost with the practices of the
monastic life, and of the order into which he
had entered, he made his way to Kent.

4. He went on also to the Eastern English
to see the institutions of the abbot Botolph,[4]
whom report had everywhere proclaimed to be
a man unique in life and erudition, and filled
with the grace of the Spirit. And then he made
his homeward journey, plentifully instructed, so
far as the brief period of his absence allowed ;
so much so, that during that time no man could
be found more learned than himself either in the
ecclesiastical or the monastic rule. Yet neither
by consideration of his priestly degree, nor by
that of his learning, nor even by that of his
birth, did he choose,[5] as some men do, to abandon
his attitude of humility ; nay rather in all things
he took pains to submit himself to regular observance. For instance, whilst he held, and that
for no short time, the office of baker, in the midst
of his duties of sifting the flour, lighting and
cleaning the oven, and baking loaves in it,
he was diligent not to omit the learning and

practice of the rites of the priesthood : nay, at this very time he was bidden to superintend the instruction of the brethren in the observance of the monastic rule, that in virtue of his innate learning united with the warmth of his inspired earnestness he might be bound both to instruct them that were ignorant and to confound them that were stubborn.

5.   But as the season drew nigh in which the heavenly Judge had decreed to make him more prominently a ruler of faithful souls, our pastor and abbot Benedict (of blessed memory), having taken knowledge of the grace of his learning, piety and diligence, when he had arranged to establish this monastery in which the loving-kindness of heaven has assembled us, succeeded in obtaining him from the bishop above mentioned as a helper and fellow - builder in the establishment of his monastery.   Not that a man so greatly skilled as Benedict needed Ceolfrid as a teacher for his own instruction.   For he had crossed the seas many times over, and had explored the regions of Gaul and Italy, nay, even those of the Islands,[6] and by this time had the statutes of the ancient monasteries by heart;

6.   in fine he was wont to say that he had learned the rule which he taught in seventeen of

the most ancient monasteries, and that all which
he had anywhere seen that was of greatest worth,
all this he had stored in the treasure-house of
his heart, had brought over to Britain, and had
delivered[7] to us to observe. But, just as the
Apostle Barnabas, though he was a good man
and full of the Holy Ghost and of faith, when
he was intending to teach at Antioch, first came
to Tarsus, where he knew that he would find
Saul, of whom he remembered, that in his first
training in the faith which he adopted he had
already given remarkable indications of virtue,
in order that, using him as a colleague, he might
fulfil, as he had designed, the ministry of the
word ; or just as Moses, elected and educated
by the Lord himself to be leader of the people
of Israel, lest, left to himself, he should tremble
to bear the burden of so vast a sovreignty, is
attended by the help of his brother Aaron, that,
assisted by him as priest and prophet, he might
fulfil the duty he had undertaken : so, no doubt
—so the famous abbot Benedict, though he was
deeply versed in all monastic lore, sought, when
he founded his monastery, the help of Ceolfrid,
who as his fellow in devotion to learning might
strengthen the observance of the regular life,
and also in his rank as a priest might accom-
plish the service of the altar.

7.   They began then to build their monastery
at the mouth of the river Wear in the six hundred and seventy-fourth year of our Lord's incarnation, the second indiction,[8] the fourth year
of King Ecgfrid, having received from him the
land, in the first instance, of fifty families ;[9] for
afterwards either by his own gift or that of other
kings and nobles it grew to more.   In the year
after the monastery had been founded Benedict
went over sea, and sought of the abbot Torthelm,
long united with him in the ties of friendship,
master - builders under whose superintendence
and by whose labour he might erect a church
of stone ; and when he had received them, he
brought them over from Gaul to Britain.

8.   Ceolfrid meanwhile grew weary of his
post as prior.[10]   The freedom of monastic peace
had more charms for him than the responsibility
of guiding others ; moreover he had to put up
with the jealousies and very bitter persecu-
tions of certain men of rank, who could not
brook the restraint of his conventual rule.   So
retiring to his own monastery he made haste
to submit himself to the lowly service of his
former mode of life : but, when Benedict followed him thither and pressed him to return,
Ceolfrid, won over at last by his affectionate

entreaties comes back to Wearmouth, and industriously carries out those regulations connected with the establishment and arrangement of the monastery which in conjunction with his friend he had already commenced.

9. As soon then as a basilica of exquisite workmanship had been very expeditiously erected and dedicated to the honour of St. Peter the Apostle, the most reverend abbot Benedict prepared for a visit to Rome ; his intention being to bring back to his country an abundance of sacred books, some sweet memorial of the relics of the blessed martyrs, a delineation of the stories in the canonical scriptures that should be well worthy of reverence," nay, as on many previous occasions, other things besides, the gifts of the world abroad, but above all else teachers to instruct his people according to the custom of the Roman use in the order of chanting and ministration in the church which he had recently founded.

10. Ceolfrid went with him on his journey, wishful to school himself more thoroughly at Rome than he could in Britain in the duties of his degree ; whilst Eosterwini, a priest, and kinsman of Benedict, was left in charge of the monastery during their absence. So, God working

with them, their intention was carried into effect. They acquaint themselves at Rome with many statutes of the church, and they bring back with them to Britain John (of blessed memory), precentor of the church in Rome, and abbot of St. Martin's,[12] who taught us abundantly the systematic rule of chanting, both by his own living voice and from the musical score.

11. Now eight years after they had begun to establish the aforesaid monastery it pleased King Ecgfrid for the redemption of his soul to grant to the most reverend abbot Benedict yet another estate—the land of forty families—that thereon a church and monastery in honour of St. Paul might be erected; not indeed cut off from union with the older monastery but in all respects bound thereto in brotherly concord. This work was committed to Ceolfrid, and he carried it out with no lack of energy. For taking with him twenty-two[13] of the brethren, ten of them tonsured, and twelve yet awaiting the grace of tonsure, he came to the place, all the buildings which the need of the monastery specially required having first been erected there,[14] and inaugurated the identical discipline of regular observance and the same complete canonical method of chanting and reading which was maintained in the older monastery ; and that

at a time when by no means all the members of
his company knew how to chant the psalms,
much less how to read in the church, or to repeat
the antiphons or responds.[15]   But what helped
them was their love of religion, and the example
of their zealous ruler, and his tactful persistency.
For, in his desire to set deep the roots of monastic observance he was generally wont to attend
the church with them at all canonical hours ; to
refresh himself and to rest when they did ; that,
if anything needed correction, if any lesson had
to be taught to the novices, he himself might be
there to perform the task.

12.   Now in the third year from the foundation of the monastery he began to build a church
to be dedicated in the name of St. Paul the
Apostle on a site, on which Ecgfrid himself had
marked out the position of the altar.   This work
grew so fast day by day, that, although the
workmen were few in number, it came to be consecrated in the year that followed its inception.

Now at the time when the most reverend
abbot Benedict had sent abbot Ceolfrid to Jarrow, he appointed also Eosterwini, whom I
mentioned above, a priest, and a kinsman of
his own, as ruler of the older monastery ; not
that one and the same monastery could or ought

to have two abbots, but, because he himself in consideration of his native wisdom and the ripeness of his counsels was wont to be somewhat frequently summoned to the royal presence, nor was there always time for him to involve himself in the management and arrangement of the concerns of his monastery. He sought therefore for a colleague, with whose assistance he might the more easily and with less anxiety support the burden of government required of him. And moreover he was hastening his departure to Rome, so as to bring home with him from abroad the good things needed for the monasteries which he had founded.

13. Now whilst he was tarrying in places beyond the sea, behold, a sudden tempest of pestilence laid hold of Britain, and wasted it with widespread disaster. In which visitation many persons from both his monasteries passed away, and the abbot Eosterwini himself (honoured and dear to God) was suddenly taken to the Lord in the fourth year of his appointment as abbot. In whose place the brethren, in agreement with the recommendation of abbot Ceolfrid, chose for their abbot Sigfrid, a deacon of the same monastery, a man of wonderful holiness, exceedingly learned in the scriptures and conspicuously devoted to their study.

14. Furthermore in the monastery over which Ceolfrid presided all those brethren who could read or preach or recite the antiphons and responds were taken away, with the exception of the abbot and one little lad, who had been reared and taught by him, and who is at this day still in the same monastery, where he holds the rank of a priest, and both by written and spoken words justly commends his teacher's praiseworthy acts to all who desire to know of them. Now he—I mean the abbot—being much distressed by reason of the aforesaid pestilence, gave command that, their former use being suspended, they should go through the whole psalter, except at vespers and matins, without the recitation of the antiphons. And, when this practice had been followed not without many tears and plaints on his own part for the space of one week, being unable to endure it longer he resolved once again that the customary order of the psalms with their antiphons should be restored; and, all endeavouring themselves thereunto, by himself and the help of the boy above mentioned with no small pains he carried out his resolve, till such time as a sufficient number of associates in the divine service could be trained up by himself or gathered from other places.

F

15. But when Benedict came home, laden as always with treasures from abroad, he was grieved indeed at the disaster that had befallen his monastery, but by no means displeased that Sigfrid, a man loveable before God, had been elected abbot in Eosterwini's place ; and he enjoined him to conduct very vigorously the charge which he had undertaken, himself lending him his aid in the duties of instruction and worship. But not long afterwards each of them falls sick, and as their sufferings gradually increased both are laid upon their beds without power to rise even into a sitting posture.

16. Consequently, after counsel taken with the brethren, Benedict summoned Ceolfrid, and appointed him abbot of both houses, commanding that they should be in all respects one monastery though situate in two places, always under the rule of one abbot, and safeguarded by the same protection of privilege ;[16] and in accordance with a clause in that same letter of privilege which he had obtained from Pope Agatho, as well as with the rule of the holy father Benedict,[17] he ordered that an abbot for this same monastery should never be sought for on the ground of consanguineous succession, but solely in respect of the character of his life and

of his diligence in teaching—a principle which he had himself followed in the appointment of Ceolfrid, who was knit to him in spiritual rather than in natural affinity, although he had a brother of his own after the flesh, in blood indeed very near to him, but by lack of heart very far estranged.

17. So Ceolfrid was appointed abbot at Wearmouth on the twelfth day of May, in the third year of King Aldfrid, the first indiction, it being the eighth year since he had founded the monastery of St. Paul. And that same year the venerable abbot and deacon Sigfrid, purified by the fires of long sickness, departed to the realms of heaven on the twenty-second day of August in the third year of his abbacy. Furthermore at the beginning of the following year, that is, on the twelfth day of January,[18] the abbot Benedict (dear to God) himself also from the furnace of prolonged weakness —wherein his practice was ever to give thanks unto God—entered into the rest and light of the celestial life, after completing the sixteenth year of his government of the monastery.

18. He had, in fact, for eight years personally acted as ruler of the monastery of St. Peter the Apostle, and for just so many years

more thereafter he had, through the agency of
Ceolfrid, devoted himself in addition to the
oversight of the monastery of St. Paul; for the
first four years of which latter period (as is above
set forth) he governed the monastery of St.
Peter with Eosterwini as his assistant; for the
three succeeding years he had Sigfrid, in the last
year Ceolfrid as his colleague in the office of ruler.
So Benedict was buried in the porch of St. Peter
at the east side of the altar, to which place also
the bones of the most reverend abbots Eosterwini and Sigfrid were subsequently translated.

19. So, when he had passed from death unto
life, Ceolfrid undertook the oversight of the two
monasteries, or rather of the one monastery
situate in two places, and maintained it with
sagacity and watchfulness for a period of
twenty-seven years. For he was a man of
acute mind, energetic in action, ardent with a
zeal for righteousness, glowing at once with
love and fear towards God, stern in chiding sin-
ners, gentle in cherishing penitents, painstaking
in the observance and teaching of the statutes of
the regular life, kindly in the relieving of poverty
and the bestowing of alms, bountiful also in mon-
netary dealings, whether in the giving of that
which was asked of him, or in the recompens-

ing of that which had been given to him, one that gave attendance to prayers and psalmody with devout regularity."[19]

20. †And so he endowed the monasteries over which he presided with good store of possessions without, and no less with others within. And that he might render them the more safe from the attacks of evil men, he sent envoys to Rome, and sought and obtained from Pope Sergius (of blessed memory) a letter of privilege after the manner of that which his predecessor Benedict had received from Agatho.[20]† For he further enriched them very abundantly with such vessels as belong to the ministry of the church and of the altar; and the collection of books which either he himself or Benedict had brought from Rome he splendidly enlarged, so that amongst other things he caused three Pandects[21] to be transcribed, two of which he placed in his two monasteries, in their churches, in order that all who wished to read any chapter of either Testament might readily find what they desired; whilst as to the third, when he was about to make his departure for Rome, he decided to present it as a gift to St. Peter, the prince of the apostles.

---

† The passage marked with daggers (††) has evidently been tampered with. *See* note.

21.   For, when, as he then was, worn out with extreme old age he saw that he could no longer set forth to his pupils the pattern of his first activity, he lit upon a counsel of utility, which was to leave the government of his monastery in younger hands, and himself as a pilgrim to draw near to the home of the apostles ; and there, set free from earthly anxieties, with unhindered application to prayer to bethink himself of his last day ; following herein the example of his brother Cynefrid, who, as we have recorded above, in pursuit of the life of contemplation gave up the charge of his monastery, and, for the Lord's sake, exchanged his fatherland for a place of self-sought exile.

22.   And so he prepared a vessel, made out a list of the envoys whom he intended to proceed to Rome, set in order the presents which were to be delivered to St. Peter, and provided a due supply of such things as were required for so long a journey. But that he himself was to be one of the party he for the time being deliberately concealed, fearing, as he did, that, if his intentions should be publicly divulged, he might either be prevented and delayed by his friends, or might at least become pecuniarily indebted to the bounty of a good many persons without having the time or the means for making them any

return. For he always preserved this characteristic of the liberal mind, that, if any gift were bestowed on him by any person, greater or less, he would certainly not allow his benefactor to depart without recompense, but generally presented him with some more substantial favour.

23. So then when all things were ready, and the day of departure was approaching, he called together into the church the brethren who were in the monastery of St. Peter, and revealed his plans. All began to weep, and falling on their faces they lay hold of his feet; with torrents of tears they beseech him not to leave them so suddenly, but to tarry with them if it were but for one day. He yielded to their entreaties, and abode with them that day and night—it was the Tuesday before Whitsunday — and in the morning with very many of them in his company he went forth to the brethren stationed in the monastery of St. Paul, talked with them, and told them how he had now arranged to leave them. As they wept aloud, much distressed about his sudden departure, he spoke gently and kindly to the whole brotherhood, asked them to observe the rule which he had taught, to continue in the fear of the Lord, and not to hinder by their entreaties and tears the journey which he had designed; and to forgive

him if he had ever transgressed the limits of moderation—for, indeed, he himself from the bottom of his heart forgave all who had offended him in any matter, and desired for them all that they should then and always find mercy with the Lord.

24. For no short while they withstood his purpose, till at last, he himself, too, shedding many a tear, induced them to give him leave to depart as was but meet with their blessing and goodwill. Only they besought him earnestly that, if he should reach the sanctuaries of the blessed apostles, he would with frequent prayers commend them to the Lord ; or, if before that might be he should pass away, that he would be ever mindful to intercede for their salvation.

25. He went forth on the same day, whether burning with desire to make his journey, or urged by weariness at the distress of the brethren, after enjoining that, with the grace of his own blessing, according to the rule of the holy father Benedict and the statutes of their privilege they should appoint for themselves as abbot that one of their own number whom they deemed most worthy. And coming back to the monastery of St. Peter, as soon as day dawned, after mass had been sung at St. Peter's and St. Mary's,

and those who were present had received the communion, he at once with mind resolved calls all the brethren into St. Peter's Church, asks for their prayers on his own behalf and himself recites a prayer ; then he sets fire to the incense, and holding the censer in his hand takes his stand on the steps from which he had been accustomed to read, and gives the kiss to very many of them, for his own grief and theirs prevented him from giving it to all. He goes forth censer in hand to the oratory of St. Laurence the Martyr, which is in the dormitory of the brethren, and they themselves follow his steps, singing the antiphon from the prophet—" The way of the righteous is made straight, and the path of the saints is prepared," and " they go from strength to strength," with the addition of the sixty-sixth Psalm,[22] "God be merciful unto us and bless us, and shew us the light of His countenance, and be merciful unto us and bless us." And then, going forth with incense kindled he once more addresses them all, bidding them to keep peace one with another, to beware of ill-feelings, ill words, and ill doings ; to expostulate with each and every sinner according to the precept of the Gospel, first man with man, then by twos and threes, and to take pains to recall such into the way of truth; and if any fruit should come of their diligence to rejoice, but if not then at last to bring forth their offences to public view; to preserve concord and brotherly unity with the brethren at St. Paul's, to remember that both houses were but one monastery, which was to be ruled continually by one abbot, lest, if the bond of brotherhood should be shattered from within, the door should be thrown open for the invasion of harm from without, as happened in the case of the people of the Hebrews, which, when by the folly of the son of Solomon it was divided against itself, never knew respite from the sword of the aliens.

26. When his address was ended the antiphon was resumed, and with it the psalm above mentioned, and they pass out to the river, leading forth their father with mournful song as one all but lost to them; and once more he gives to each and all the kiss of peace, their chant again and again interrupted by their tears, and having recited a prayer on the shore he ascends the vessel and sits down at its prow. The deacons seated themselves beside him, one of them holding a golden cross which he had made, the other lighted candles.

27. As the vessel sped across the river, he

gazed on the brethren who were bewailing his
departure, and, as he listened to the glorious
music blending itself with sorrow-laden song he
could in no wise restrain himself from sobs
and tears. But this alone he repeated with frequent ejaculation—"Christ, have mercy on that
company! Almighty Lord, defend that band!
yea I know it in very truth—I never found any
better than they, more ready to yield obedience
. . . Christ, my God, protect them." Thus
he quitted the vessel ; bows before the cross,
mounts his horse—and departed. He laid aside
the anxieties of this world's concerns, hastening
from even his kindred English people to be a
pilgrim from land to land ; that with mind more
free and pure he might dedicate himself to the
contemplation of the angelic societies of heaven.

28. The brethren returned to the church,
and, prayers being ended, they discuss what is
to be done. They decided that with prayer and
fasting they should ask of the Lord whom they
should set over themselves as abbot. But inasmuch as their venerable father had at his departure enjoined that none of them should fast
on the day of his journeying—nay, rather that
all should hold greater festival—and on that account had bidden some of his comrades to tarry
with them till the morning meal was ended—

(now it was the Thursday preceding Whitsunday)—it was resolved that fast should be observed on the following day and night, and
that on the Saturday they should refresh themselves at the third hour after noon only, and
that because by reason of the vigil preceding
the Sunday's solemnities they could no further
prolong their fasting : on the other hand they
arranged that at the usual canonical hours of
prayer the number of their psalms should be in
no slight degree augmented; and also that they
should all beseech the Eternal Lovingkindness,
that, on the day when by the coming of the
Holy Spirit He vouchsafed to hallow the birth-
day of His own church, now unto themselves
also, that were truly a portion of that church, by
the grace of that same Spirit a worthy ruler
might be revealed.

29.   Matters being thus settled there came
thither from the monastery of St. Paul on Whitsunday very many of the brethren stationed
there.   And all with one consent selected
Hwaetbercht to be ordained in the abbot's
stead, who from his very early years had dwelt
in the same monastery,[23] and, having been fully
trained both in ecclesiastical and monastic learning, by this time already exercised influence in
his degree as a priest.   He then at once as

abbot elect wrote a letter to the apostolic pope
in commendation of his father and predecessor,
and made ready presents to send therewith.
Then following the steps of Ceolfrid in company with certain of the brethren he found him
in the monastery of Albert, in a place which
is called Valehorn,[24] read the letter to him, and
set before him the gifts which he was to deliver.

30. Ceolfrid gladly welcomed the choice of
the brethren and confirmed it with his own
benediction, and gave full instructions to Hwaetbercht in many points, as to how he should preside as ruler of the monastery. The letter
alluded to began thus :—

To the well beloved lord in our Lord
and thrice blessed pope, Gregory. Hwaetbercht, your lowly servant, abbot of the
monastery of the most blessed Peter, prince
of the Apostles in the land of the Saxons,[25]
perpetual health in the Lord.

I do not cease to give thanks to the providence of the heavenly judgment —I and
my holy brethren, who in these parts, for
the finding of rest unto their souls desire
to bear the most sweet yoke of Christ—in

that in these our times it hath vouchsafed in thy person to appoint so glorious a vessel of election to the oversight of the whole church ; in order that by this light of faith and truth, with which thou thyself art filled of God, it might abundantly besprinkle with the ray of its lovingkindness all that are of lower degree. We commend then to thy sacred benignity, wellbeloved father and lord in Christ, the venerable grey hairs of our wellbeloved father, to wit, the abbot Ceolfrid, foster-father and guardian of the spiritual liberty and peace which we have in monastic retirement. And first indeed we render thanks to the holy and undivided Trinity, for that he himself, though he has departed from us not without very great grief, wailing, and lamentation on our part, and not without the attendance of our tears, has yet passed to the sacred joys of his long desired rest. For now, even when grown weary with old age, he has in his devotion sought once more that home of the blessed Apostles, which, when he recalled it to mind, he used always to rejoice that he had in the days of his youth visited, seen, and adored; and after the long labours and incessant anxi-

eties of more than forty years, in which,
by right of his abbacy, he has presided
with a love of virtue, elsewhere unequalled,
over the monasteries subject to his rule,
as[26] one just summoned to the society of
the heavenly life, worn out with years far
advanced, and almost at the point of death,
he begins once more to be a pilgrim for
Christ's sake, that so the old thorns of worldly cares may be with less hindrance consum-
ed in the spiritual furnace by the glowing
fires of contrition. Then further we beseech
your fatherhood, that—what we have been
unworthy to do—your diligence may render him the last acts of lovingkindness ;
knowing this for certain, that, though you
have his body, yet we, and you with us,
have his consecrated spirit, whether tarrying in the body or set free from its bonds,
as a mighty intercessor for our transgres-
sions and an advocate before the lovingkindness of heaven.

31. Ceolfrid set forth then from his monastery on the fourth day of June, being Thursday,
intending to sail down to the sea by the mouth
of the river Humber. On the fourth day of
July, being a Saturday, he embarked on a vessel, which, before it reached the coast of Gaul,

was brought to land in three several provinces, in each of which he was by all persons honourably received, and treated with veneration, as one who had determined by the setting of an incomparable example of virtue to crown the grace of his long and holy life.

32. On the completion of his voyage he reached the mainland of Gaul on Wednesday the twelfth day of August, and in those parts too he was splendidly honoured by all persons, and specially by King Hilperic[27] himself, who, besides the gifts which he offered him, further gave him letters of commendation through all the provinces of his kingdom, bidding that he should be everywhere received peaceably, and that none should presume to hinder him in his journey. Moreover he commended him, and with him all his party, to the kindly hospitalities of Liudbrand,[28] king of the Lombards. So he came to Langres, a city of the Burgundians, on Friday, the twenty-fifth day of September; and there worn out as much by length of days as by sickness—yea, as the Scriptures use to say, failing in a good old age, he was gathered unto his fathers. For he had lived seventy-four years, of which he had spent forty-seven in the office of the priesthood, and thirty-five in the position of independent abbot.

33. Now he left in his monasteries a band of soldiers of Christ more than six hundred in number : and moreover an estate that according to the customary English reckoning might support one hundred and fifty families. From the date of his departure from his monastery down to his very last day, besides the psalms appointed for the canonical hours, he daily chanted the psalter of David in order three times over, thus exceeding his original practice, continued through many years, of running through the psalter twice daily, and on no day did he omit to offer before the Lord the sacrifice of the holy oblation on behalf of himself and of his friends—even when through excessive weakness he could not ride, and had to be carried in a horse litter—save only on that one day when, his vessel being driven by the storms, he was all day long tossing upon the sea, and also on the four days that immediately preceded his death.

34. There were in his company about eighty men drawn from various parts, who all of them followed him in a body and honoured him as their father. For he had given orders to his attendants, that, if they found any of his companions without means of support, they should

G

give him at once either food or money. For
indeed he was naturally kind-hearted, and one
that had a special reverence for the poor.
Consequently when he was to leave, and when
he was actually leaving, his monastery, the
common lamentation of the needy and the
wanderers bore witness that in him they had
lost, as it were, a father and sustainer. This
type of virtue he was diligently careful to culti-
vate, not only as being commended to his heart
by the fear and love of God, but also as descend-
ing to him from a parent by hereditary right.
For his own father, when he was holding the
very honourable position of a king's thane,[29]
always took such great pleasure in showing
works of mercy towards the poor, that on one
occasion, when he had prepared a very splendid
banquet for the reception of the king, and some
sudden necessity connected with warfare chanced
to prevent his coming, the good man gave thanks
to the divine providence, and forthwith bade all
the poor, the strangers, the feeble folk of the
neighbourhood to be called to the feast ; and
with that bounty, wherewith he had intended to
entertain an earthly king and his attendants, he
entertained, in the persons of His lowly followers,
the King most High, having respect unto an
eternal reward ; devoting himself to attendance

on his male guests, and bidding his wife to fulfil
in all things amongst the women the personal
service of the lowliest of handmaidens.

35. Ceolfrid arrived then at Langres about
nine o'clock in the morning on the day above
stated—the twenty-fifth of September, at the
beginning of the fifteenth indiction : and coming to his haven in the suburbs of that same
city was received with rejoicing by Gangwulf,[30]
the lord of those regions : for he had met him
previously on the road and invited him thither,
and also given him instructions that he should
be kindly received, even if he himself should not
be present. He earnestly besought his guest
not to leave him till he should be restored to
health, but, if God should so will it, to await
there at the tombs of the holy martyrs his
entrance into the heavenly life.

36. Now it came to pass that on the very
day of his arrival about four o'clock in the after-
noon he departed to the Lord. The next morning accompanied by a long procession, both of
his own followers and of those resident in the
neighbourhood of that city, his body was borne
about three miles distance to the monastery of
this same Gangwulf which lay about a mile

and a half to the south of the town. It was
buried in the church of the holy trine martyrs,
Speusippus, Eleosippus, and Meliosippus, who
being born of one mother at one birth were in
the days of old crowned there with martyrdom,
and buried in the same place as their grand-
mother, Leonella, who had herself likewise borne
a martyr's witness at her departure from the
body.

37. So then when their father had been
buried some of the brethren of his escort returned home to tell in his own monastery where
and when he had departed from the body ; and
some on the other hand completed their journey
to Rome, to deliver the presents which he had
sent. Amongst which presents there was of
course the Pandect which we mentioned, derived from its Hebrew and Greek originals by
the translation of St. Jerome the priest, a volume which has at its commencement certain
verses written in this wise :—

Where in due pomp high Peter's corse hath rest,
Chief o'er the church by faith profound confest,
I, Abbot Ceolfrid, from the furthest end
Of English soil my heart's vowed tribute send;
So, when our Prince unbars of bliss the gate,
Heaven's lasting home shall me and mine await.[31]

38. There were moreover some of Ceolfrid's followers, who through attachment to their father, there buried, chose to remain in this same city of Langres; these, however, afterwards accomplished their intention and desire of reaching Rome. And so great was the favour shown by Gangwulf to the companions of our most reverend abbot, that he entertained them all after the funeral at a magnificent banquet; and for those who were departing whether in this or that direction he granted both guides and supplies for the way; whilst in addition to this he appointed a provision for those who remained on the spot so long as they chose to stay there.

39. Concerning Ceolfrid and his presents what the apostolic pope thought is testified by his letter of reply, which commences in this way :—

Gregory the bishop, servant of the servants of God, to the religious abbot Hwaetbercht.

We have by perusal understood the drift of the letter of your own worthy and religious personality. You show that you rejoice with the Truth (by whose grace

those things which are not are called as
though they were) in the matter of our
promotion ; and to the authority of our
apostolical prerogative, the ministry of
which we, however unworthily, discharge,
you are most ready to bow. For which
things' sake know, that you ought, as our
fellow-workman, to pray the more instantly,
and that with continual supplications, that
he, whose presidency you welcome, may be
able to prove a blessing to himself and to
you and to many : and know further, that
he, whose venerable grey hairs (hallowed
unto God) you have taken pains to commend to our care, has, before we could
receive him, been translated at the divine
call from things temporal unto those eternal,
yet not before he had to his own lasting
remembrance sent a present to the Lord
and to our common patron St. Peter, chief
lord of the Apostles. We, approving his
faith shown in the bestowal of his gift,
have deemed him worthy of perpetual
commemoration, and pray that this well
approved instructor in holy and monastic
ordinances may live before God as a fore-
runner of worthy disciples ; so that the
grace of heaven, which has taken him to

itself, may by the perfecting of his merits
number him with Aaron and Moses, those
holy leaders of the people of God withdrawn from service as they made their way
to the land of promise, and with that holy
Elijah, so swiftly snatched away to the
skies. And we pray that his pupil that
survives and succeeds to his office, together
with the comrades whom he is called to rule,
may be by the same grace with the spiritual
gifts of that choicest leader Joshua, of
Phinehas, and of Elisha, more than liberally
equipped.[32] Fare thou well.

40. Now the companions of our father (dear
unto God) who came back to us used to tell us,
that on the night after his venerable body was
committed to its tomb, while three wardens of
the church were, according to custom, keeping
watch over it by night, the scent[33] of a marvellous odour filled the whole church : then there
followed a light, which itself also lasting for no
short period arose at length to the roof of the
church. The men went forth very quickly, and
as they gazed on it beheld that same light rap-
idly ascending to the heavens, so that by its
brilliancy all the lands around were illumined
as with the light of day. By which means it

was given them to understand plainly that the ministers of eternal light and abiding sweetness had been there to consecrate by their visitation the resting place of that holy form. And hence a custom grew amongst the inhabitants of that place, that at the several times of daily or nightly prayers, when the canonical service of psalmody was concluded, all the male worshippers should bend their knees in supplication at his tomb. Yea, and beside this, the report of other signs and healings wrought thereat hath been spread abroad by the grace of Him whose wont it is to prosper His saints in the warfare of this life, and to crown them as conquerors in the life which is to come, [even Jesus Christ our Lord, who, with the Father and the Holy Ghost, liveth and reigneth world without end.[34]] Amen.

NOTES.

(The letter P in brackets [P] followed by figures denoting volume and page, signifies that the statement made is derived from Mr. Plummer's notes, many of which give fuller and further information, which will be found of value to the more advanced student.)

1. (Exordium). The text reads *cepit* (i.e. coepit) *arsumere*. There is a confusion between two words meaning respectively "took" and "began." Hence probably the addition of another verb to complete the sense—*assumere* "to take to himself," omitted by the present editor.

2. (§ 1.)—The life they lived.—Referred to its Greek original (Hebr. xiii. 7), and to the verb connected therewith. The expression used implies the life of a man as his neighbours saw it.

3. (§ 2.)—Students of Scripture in Ireland.—In the period to which our work refers many Englishmen visited Ireland for the purpose of study. Bede enumerates frequent instances. A letter of Aldhelm, Bishop of Sherborne (705—709), describes the English students in that country as "a swarm of bees." The subjects studied were grammar, geometry, physics, and the allegorical interpretation of Scripture. [P II. 196.]

4. (§ 4.)—Botolph—from whom Boston (Botolph's town) derives its name.

5. (§ 4.)—reading "maluit" in place of "valuit."

6. (§ 5.)—The islands—i.e. of Lérins, a group of Islands off the coast of Cannes, where, according to Bede's *Lives of the Abbots* (§ 2), Biscop spent two years of his life. [P II. 357.]

7. (§ 6.)—reading "tradiderat."

8. (§ 7.)—Indiction—cycles of fifteen years, the origin of which is unknown. There were three modes of reckoning : (1) The Constantinopolitan, beginning on September 1 ; (2) The Cæsarean, which began on September 24 ; (3) The Roman, commencing with December 25 or January 1. The author of our work used the Cæsarean system (see § 35), and so also did Bede. His rule for finding the indiction is as follows : Take the year of Our Lord, add to it the number three, and divide by fifteen ; the remainder is the indiction. If there is no remainder, the date is the fifteenth indiction. [P II. 38, 39.]

9. (§ 7.)—Land of families—otherwise called "hides." The measurement varied according to the quality of the land, and the economic condition of the neighbourhood [P II. 40, 41.] Our author describes King Ecgfrid's gift as "the land of forty families;" the number stated in Bede's *Lives of the Abbots* is seventy.

10. (§ 9.)—Prior.—Used in the sense commonly understood in the middle ages, i.e. the person acting under the abbot as second in authority.

11. (§ 9.)—Pictures in churches.—Bede in his *Lives of the Abbots* (§§ 6 and 9), gives a detailed account of these. At St. Peter's Church the ceiling was adorned with pictures of the Virgin and the twelve Apostles; the Gospel story was represented on the south side of the church, and that of the Apocalypse was displayed on the northern wall. The tale of Our Lord's life was portrayed in the church of St. Mary at Monkwearmouth. At Jarrow were exhibited a double series of type below and antitype above; two instances are mentioned (1) Isaac carrying the wood, and Christ bearing his cross; (2) Moses' serpent in the wilderness, and the Son of Man on His cross.

12. (§ 10.)—John the chanter.—Further information concerning him is given in Bede's *Ecclesiastical History,* iv. 18, where we are told that he was instructed by Pope Agatho to bring back a report as to the orthodoxy of the Church in England in regard to the doctrine of the human and divine wills in Christ. He died at Turin on his return, but his report was sent on to Rome and approved as satisfactory.

13. (§ 11.)—The first occupants of the monastery at Jarrow.— Bede gives the number as seventeen. The confusion is between xxii and xvii. [P II. 361.]

14. (§ 11.)—The Harleian text reads, "primis autumni abscessum," which is obviously corrupt. The original text "would apparently have given us a more precise date for the foundation of Jarrow." [P II. 372.] An ancient gloss may have crept in, such as "in primis diebus autumni abscesserunt,"— "they went forth in the first days of autumn."

15. (§ 11.)—Antiphons and responds.—The daily services of a monastery at the canonical hours are the original sources of the Mattins and Evensong of the English Prayer Book, which in its preface "concerning the services of the Church" explains the meaning of the above terms. The antiphons were meant to give to the psalms the special colouring required for day or season, or to mark the break between succeeding psalm. One such antiphon we have retained in the "Gloria Patri" between psalm and psalm. "Responds were similarly used in connection with the lections." [P].

16. (§ 16.)—Letters of privilege. — The object of these was generally more or less independence from episcopal control

or interference. Bede *(Lives of the Abbots* § 6), whose relations with at least one bishop were extremely intimate and friendly, reckons the grant of a letter of privilege as a minor advantage gained to his monastery. The effect of it in the present case, seems to have been to secure to the monks of Wearmouth and Jarrow (after the founder's death) the right to nominate their own abbots, the confirmation of their choice by the formal benediction of the bishop being still required. Such was the method pursued in the case of the election of Hwaetbercht. (See Bede's *Lives* § 20).

17. (§ 16.) — Benedict. — i.e. Benedict of Nursia. (See Introduction.)

18. (§ 17.) — See chronological note below.

19. (§ 19.) — Omission. — The opening words of § 20 lead us to infer that the preceding paragraph has lost one or more of its concluding sentences, viz., those which described additions made to the landed estates of the monastery. The information here missing (or some of it) is to be found in the contemporary work of Bede (§ 15): the land of eight families near the river Fresca (the position of which is unknown) was received from King Aldfrid in exchange for a history of the world, which Biscop had bought at Rome; in exchange for this land with further money paid King Osred gave the land of twenty families at Sambuce (possibly Cambois in Northumberland); the land of twenty families at Dalton was also secured to the monastery, the gift of Witmaer, who himself became a monk at St. Peter's: and in the same list Bede rightly places pope Sergius' letter of privilege.

20. (§ 20.) — The words within daggers belong to the lost passage above mentioned. Their insertion here interferes with the construction of the paragraph.

21. (§ 20.) — Pandects. — The word here used is of Greek origin and signifies a comprehensive collection of learning. It was first applied to Justinian's complete code of laws; afterwards to the Holy Scriptures of the Old and New Testaments. [P II. 365.]

22. (§ 26.) — The sixty-sixth Psalm — known to us as the sixty-seventh. The vulgate numeration is different, Psalms ix. and x. being reckoned (and correctly so) as one psalm.

23. (§ 29.) — Hwaetbercht. — The language appears to imply that he was an inmate of the monastery at Jarrow.

24. (§ 29.) — Valehorn. — The situation is unknown. [P.]

25. (§ 30.) — Land of the Saxons. — The document including this word occurs also in Bede's *Lives.* It is "the only instance in which any name derived from the invading Teutonic tribes is given to this island or any part of it; elsewhere it is always Britain. And though Northumbria was purely Anglian, the

name used is not 'Anglia,' but 'Saxonia.'" [P II. 368.] This is, however, in accordance with the usage of the Highlanders of Scotland, with whom every Englishman is a Sassenach, or Saxon.

26. (§ 30.)—reading "quasi."

27. (§ 32.)—Hilperic.—Chilperic II., King of Neustria, 715—720 [P], or Northern France. Out of this kingdom grew eventually the kingdom of France. Chilperic was one of the last sovereigns of the degenerate Merovingian dynasty.

28. (§ 32.)—Liudbrand.—King of the Lombards, 712—744 [P], a Teutonic race, who occupied northern Italy in 567. Their kingdom was overthrown by Charles the Great in the year 744.

29. (§ 34.)—Ceolfrid's father obtained nobility by becoming a member of the "comitatus," or body of king's comrades, commonly called thanes. Their status is fully described in Green's *History of the English People,* I. 35.

30. (§ 35.)—Gangwulf.—Nothing further is known of him. [P].

31. (§ 37.)—These verses led to the discovery of the famous *Codex Amiatinus,* fully treated of in the Appendix to this work.

32. (§ 39.)—The text of this letter is exceedingly corrupt. An effort nevertheless has been made to translate it. The following emendation of its closing lines is suggested:—"Iesu electissimi ducis ac Finees Heliseique ditatum carismatibus indulgentius perornet."

33. (§ 40.)—reading "fragrantia."

34. (§ 40.)—Doxology.—This is found, not in the earlier, but in the later manuscript. Genuine or otherwise, it fitly concludes the sermon.

CHRONOLOGICAL NOTE.

(A refers to the anonymous *Life of Ceolfrid;* B to Bede's *Lives of the Abbots.* The numbers attached to these symbols indicate the chapters.)

The subject of the early chronology of the monastery at Wearmouth and Jarrow presents certain difficulties which to some have seemed inexplicable. It has therefore been reserved for special treatment.

1. The one certain date from which we may reckon all the rest is the resignation of Ceolfrid on 16 June, 716. We turn to B 22 and find it there stated that he served in the office of an abbot 35 years (with this A 32 agrees); or rather, the author goes on to say, 43 years from the time when Biscop began to found his monastery. The inference is that the monastery at Wearmouth was founded in 673.

2. Again, we are told in B 15 that Ceolfrid presided over the united monastery for 28 years, i.e., from 688 to 716. On the other hand A 19 asserts that he conducted its affairs for 27 years, but at the same time states that the period referred to begins with the death of Biscop. This took place, as both narratives affirm, in the year following Ceolfrid's formal appointment, which event is obviously B's starting point. There is then no contradiction here; it is simply the case that the two writers reckon from different points of time. Ceolfrid was abbot of the whole monastery *de jure* for 28 years, *de facto* for 27 years. He was appointed in 688, and Biscop died in 689. From this last mentioned date we may easily trace another step backward. We do so under the guidance of both our writers, who alike tell us (A 17 ; B 14) that Biscop ruled his monastery for 16 years. The conclusion is once more that the monastery was founded in the year 673.

3. But here we are met by an apparent contradiction on the part of B. The writer tells us (B 4) that Biscop *made* a monastery at the mouth of the river Wear in the year 674, the second indiction, the fourth year of King Ecgfrid. That this king's reign began on 15 February, 671 (not 670) is proved beyond question in Mr. Plummer's note on Bede's *Ecclesiastical History,* iv. 5 (Vol. II. p. 211). The indiction ended with September 23. Between these dates, then, in the year 674, Biscop made his monastery. He made it in the building season of the year, between February 15 and September 23. He did not build St. Peter's church at this time—so both writers are careful to tell us : that came later ; but he built a monastery, that is, a habitation for his monks. The order of his work is precisely that pursued at Jarrow some few years later.

4. We now proceed to find, if we can, what Biscop was about in the year 673. We learn from B 4, that on returning from Rome to Britain after one of his Continental journeys he purposed to

visit Wessex, but changed his mind on hearing that the king of that country had *at that very time* died. Now King Conwalh died, according to the Saxon Chronicle, in 672. Biscop consequently revised his plans, and came north to visit King Ecgfrid, with whom he may well have been during some months of the year 673. He told the king his history, revealed his interests, and set forth his desires ; he showed him the books and relics which he had brought from abroad. And so pleased was the king with what he heard and saw, that he *at once* gave him the estate at Wearmouth and ordered him to make a monastery there. This then is what Biscop was doing in 673. It was the first and most important matter of all. He was obtaining a site and an endowment for his monastery. This would be done in some formal and binding manner. The land would be conveyed probably by charter. The grant would be from the king to Biscop as abbot and founder of the proposed house. And so took place the real *foundation* of the monastery as an establishment, from which, as we maintain, its after history was dated. The *making*, or *building* of the monastery was a second step, and this was effected, as we are directly told, in 674. But the monastery was *founded,* as we believe, in 673. It will be well, however, to test this date by further reference to both our authorities.

5. To take first the evidence of B, the sum total of its dates and computations (to be found in B 8, 14, 15, and 22) is as follows :—(1) Biscop was abbot 8 years by himself, 4 years with Eosterwini, 3 years with Sigfrid, 1 year with Ceolfrid. (2) Ceolfrid was abbot 7 years at Jarrow, 28 years over both monasteries ; 35 years in all, or, if you count the years when he first presided under the founder, 43 years. All this may and must have been the case, if the foundation took place in 673.

6. We turn next to the statements made by A (17, 18, 19, and 32). These amount to this much :—(1) Biscop was abbot 16 years, without and with assistants, precisely as is affirmed in B 14. (2) Ceolfrid presided over both houses for 27 years after the death of Biscop, and was an abbot bearing personal rule for 35 years. He was put in charge of the whole monastery in the third year of King Aldfrid (i.e. between 21 May, 687, and 20 May, 688, both dates included ; in the first indiction (i.e., in 688) and on the 12th day of May. He had previously been 7 years at Jarrow, which was founded 8 years after Wearmouth. Again we are brought back to the year 673.

7. One other point deserves brief notice. We are told in A 17 that the appointment of Ceolfrid as sole abbot took place in the eighth year of the *foundation* of Jarrow ; in other words Jarrow was founded before 12 May, 681. The foundation was no doubt exactly similar in character to that of Wearmouth, the nature of which has been already described. Then came the building of the monastery ; so that it was not till more than two years after the foundation that St. Paul's church was commenced (A 12). This took more than a year in building, and its dedication consequently took place, as described on the original dedication-stone, in the fourth year of Ceolfrid's abbacy ; the precise day is specified as being April 23, in the 15th year of Ecgfrid, that is, as we have every reason to believe, Sunday, 23 April, 685.

APPENDIX I.

THE CODEX AMIATINUS:
WHEN AND WHERE WRITTEN.

1. *The Guardian,* February 16th, March 2nd. London, 1887.
2. *The Academy,* February 26th, March 5th. London, 1887.
3. Venerabilis Bedæ Opera Historica ad fidem Codicum Manuscriptorum recensuit Josephus Stevenson. English Historical Society.
   Vita beatorum Abbatum, Benedicti, Ceolfridi, &c.
   Historia Abbatum Gyrvensium, Auctore anonymo (Appendix). London, 1841.

There is in the Laurentian or Mediceo-Laurentian Library at Florence, a manuscript of the whole Bible in Latin, which has long been recognised by critical scholars as the oldest[1] and best copy of the Latin version of St. Jerome, commonly called the Vulgate. It is in fact one of the chief ornaments of that collection. It has recently been established beyond any doubt that this book was written at Wearmouth or Jarrow, under the superintendence of the Abbat Ceolfrid, the instructor of the Venerable Bede, and that it was intended by the Abbat as a gift to the See of St. Peter at Rome. We propose in the following pages to give a brief narrative of the various steps by which this discovery has been made, passing by for the present all critical details. Our readers will find it to be truly a marvellous history. It may not be amiss, however, first to give some account

of St. Ceolfrid himself, whose history is most interesting, and in some passages affecting.   There are two
authorities for his life besides what we are told concerning him in Bede's *Ecclesiastical History*.[2]   The first is
Bede's own most beautiful work, *The Lives of the Abbats
of Wearmouth and Jarrow*.[3]   The second is an anonymous tract, evidently written by a monk of Wearmouth
or Jarrow.   It also is inscribed in printed copies, *The
Lives of the Abbats*, but it is really a life of St. Ceolfrid,
the others being noticed only so far as their history was
connected with his.[4]   It supplies some particulars not
to be found in Bede.

St. Ceolfrid, whose name, Alban Butler says,[5] is the
same as Galfrid, Gaufrid, or Geoffrey, was born of noble
and religious parents about the year 642, seven years
after the arrival of St. Aidan, and about 30 before the
birth of his illustrious pupil, the Venerable Bede.[6]   His
father was a " comes," or ealdorman, high in the service of the King, and was even more distinguished by
his piety and kindness to the poor than by his social
position.   On one occasion,[7] in expectation of a visit
from the King, he had prepared a magnificent banquet;
but the exigencies of war having called the King away
in another direction, all his costly preparations seemed
to be rendered useless.   To most men this would have
been a dire disappointment, but, far from murmuring,
the good man gave thanks to Him who ordereth all
things rightly, then called together the poor and the
afflicted from far and near, and offered the banquet,
which he had prepared for his earthly sovereign, to the
King of Heaven in the persons of His poor members.
He waited on the men himself, while his wife served the
women, thus affording a notable instance of the change
the Gospel had wrought, even so soon, in our fierce and

haughty forefathers. From his early days Ceolfrid had striven to lead a godly life, and at the age of 18[8] he resolved to give himself up entirely to the service of God. It is hardly necessary to say that in those rough days, when war was almost the only employment for a layman, especially for a nobleman, a Monastery was the only resource for a devout youth. At Gilling, near Richmond, in Yorkshire, there was a Monastery founded by King Oswy at the instance of his gentle Queen Eanfleda, as an act of penitence for the foul murder of King Oswin. Till recently this house had been under the charge of Cynifrid, Ceolfrid's elder brother, but zeal in the pursuit of divine learning had drawn Cynifrid away to Ireland. His successor was his kinsman Tunberct, afterwards first Bishop of Hexham. Hither it was that Ceolfrid directed his steps. Perhaps we may infer from this that he was a native of Yorkshire. Being kindly received by his kinsman, Ceolfrid gave himself up with all his energy to reading, working, and to learning his monastic duties. After a time Tunberct and Ceolfrid, with some others of the brethren, were invited[9] by the famous Wilfrid, then Bishop of York, to his Monastery at Ripon, and there, in his 27th year, Ceolfrid was ordained priest by Wilfrid. He now paid a visit to Kent, to perfect himself in the monastic rules and the duties of the priesthood. He also visited with a like purpose the Abbat Botulf[10] at Ikanhoe, in Lincolnshire, from whom the town of Boston (Botulf's Town) derives its name, a man, we are told, who was everywhere famous for his singularly good life as well as his learning,—"a man full of the Holy Spirit." Having profited as much as he could by a short visit, Ceolfrid returned home, and thinking more of the duty of humility than of his worldly

H

rank, of his learning, or of his station as a Priest, he hesitated not to employ himself in the menial services of the Monastery. He became baker to the community, and was employed in winnowing corn, in kindling and cleansing the oven, and baking the bread. So were the English of that day, who thought all such work degrading, taught the dignity of labour, when they saw a man of noble birth, of great learning, and a Priest, so employing himself. While thus engaged, he was at the same time most assiduous in learning and practising all the duties of the Priesthood ; and in time, on account of his learning, the fervour of his godly zeal in instructing the ignorant, and dealing wisely with the obstinate, he was appointed to a high charge in the Monastery.

It was about this time that Benedict Biscop was planning the foundation of the famous Abbey of Wearmouth. This remarkable man had three times[11] made a journey to Rome, and had, in his visits to no less than 17[12] most ancient and famous monasteries, acquainted himself with the rules and the details of the monastic life. In these journeys Benedict had not only seen much that was interesting and instructive, but he had also collected great numbers of books, and relics, and ecclesiastical ornaments. When he came home he gave an account of all to King Ecgfrid,[13] who was so much pleased with what Benedict had to tell him, and to show him, that he made him a large grant of land at the mouth of the River Wear, on which to build a Monastery. Upon this Benedict, having heard much of Ceolfrid's learning and devotion, and skill in government, sought and obtained him from Wilfrid as a fellow worker in his new enterprise.[14] Ceolfrid therefore removed to Wearmouth. After the Monastery was erected Benedict crossed the sea to Gaul, to find masons to build a Church to be

named in honour of St. Peter. During his absence
Ceolfrid began to tire of his work. Some young noble-
men in the Monastery gave him a great deal of trouble
by their intractability and reluctance to submit to regular discipline ; so he gave up his charge and withdrew
to Ripon, whence he had come. Benedict, however, on
his return, followed him, and prevailed on him to come
back. Benedict brought not only masons from Gaul,[15]
but also workers in glass, who, besides glazing the win-
dows of the Church, taught the English the art of working in glass, of which they had previously been entirely
ignorant.[16]

When St. Peter's Church was finished, Benedict, taking Ceolfrid with him, set out on a fourth journey to
Rome.[17] Here Ceolfrid had the opportunity of vastly
increasing his stores of knowledge. They returned
laden with books, pictures, and ecclesiastical furniture,
bringing with them also John, the "archicantor," or
precentor, of St. Peter's at Rome, that he might intro-
duce the knowledge of Church music into the North of
England.

And now Ecgfrid made a further[18] donation of land
at the mouth of the Tyne, for the foundation of a new
Monastery. This was Jarrow, and thither Ceolfrid was
sent with a number of monks to begin the new establishment, which, we are constantly reminded, was not a
separate community, but formed part of the one Society
in two places. When the Monastery had been built at
Jarrow, and a Church, which was named in honour of
St. Paul, as the Church of Wearmouth had been in
honour of St. Peter, Benedict, designing a fifth journey
to Rome, appointed Ceolfrid to the charge of Jarrow,
and a young nobleman named Eosterwini, his own
cousin, to that of Wearmouth. He then set out for

Rome, and in due time came back, as usual, with a rich cargo of books and pictures, and Church furniture for the adornment of his two Monasteries. Heavy tidings awaited him on his return.

His friend King Ecgfrid had been slain in battle. A pestilence had visited Wearmouth and Jarrow and carried off many of the brethren. At Wearmouth Eosterwini had died, and the Deacon Sigfrid had, to Benedict's entire satisfaction, been chosen in his room. The account of Jarrow is most interesting, though peculiarly sad.[19] All who could read or preach, or chant the antiphons and responsories had been cut off, save the Abbat and one little boy, "who had been brought up and educated by him, and even to this time." adds the writer, "holds in the same Monastery the rank of Presbyter, esteemed by all who know him both for his discourses and his writings." These two, with many tears, sang the Canonical Hours only, save at Matins and Vespers, omitting the antiphons. This went on for a week, and then they could bear it no longer. They resumed their old practice, which they continued under all difficulties till others could be trained to take part with them. There can be no doubt that the boy was the Venerable Bede, who, by his own account, had been entrusted to Benedict at the age of seven, and by him put under the charge of Ceolfrid.[20] He would now be about 14 years of age. We are indebted to the anonymous monk for this story. It is thoroughly in accordance with Bede's character that he makes no mention of it.

Not long after this Benedict was attacked by paralysis.[21] He lingered on for three years, entirely disabled in the lower parts of his body. Sigfrid also was afflicted by an acute and incurable disease of the lungs,[22] and was drawing near his end. In these circumstances

it seemed good to Benedict and Sigfrid, with the advice
and consent of the community, to appoint Ceolfrid sole
Abbat of the united Monasteries. Bede gives a most
affecting account of the death-bed scenes[23] of Sigfrid
and of Benedict, who died about four months after his
friend and colleague.

After this Ceolfrid ruled the community for 28 years.[24]
Bede tells us that he " carried on with undiminished zeal
all the good works which his predecessor had begun
with such earnestness and energy. He built new ora-
tories, he increased the number of the vessels of the
Altar and the Church, and of vestments of every kind.
The library which Benedict had taken such pains to
found, with no less zeal he doubled in extent ; and to
one Pandect[25] of the old translation which he had
brought from Rome, he added three Pandects of the
new translation. One of these, when as an old man he
was going back to Rome, he took with him among other
things, as a gift ; two of them he left to the two Monasteries, one to each." Ceolfrid set out on his journey
to Rome in the year 716, when he was 74 years of age.
The account of his leave-taking is most picturesque, but
must be passed over here. He never reached Rome, but
died at Langres, in France. He was accompanied by
a very large retinue of no less than 80 persons. Of
these some returned home to tell what had happened,
some remained in the place where their beloved father
had been laid to rest, while others proceeded on the
journey to Rome, bearing with them the gifts that Ceolfrid had brought, and among the rest the Pandect of the
new translation.

We come now, at last, to the famous manuscript at
Florence, known as the *Codex Amiatinus,* having once
belonged to the Convent of Monte Amiata. It has long

been known and highly admired and esteemed by critical
scholars. The Bishop of Salisbury thus speaks of it:[26]

"The great Bible of Monte Amiata, now one of the
most prominent ornaments of the Mediceo-Laurentian
Library at Florence, is at once a most important speci-
men of palæography and one of the principal founda-
tions of the text of any critical edition of the version of
St. Jerome, both in the Old and New Testaments. . . .
It is a book measuring about 50 by 34 centim. (19·7 by
13·4 in.) in length and breadth, and nearly 20 centim.
(7·9 in.) in thickness without the binding; containing
1,029 leaves of beautiful vellum, written in two columns
to a page, with 43 or 44 lines to a column, in short lines,
technically called cola and commata, or sometimes, perhaps less correctly, stichi, which represent an ancient
system of punctuation perfectly intelligible to the trained
eye."

It is no wonder that curiosity should be very much
alive as to the origin and history of such a volume.
The only guides afforded by itself are:—1. A somewhat barbarous Greek inscription at the end of the prologue to the Book of Leviticus

(Ο ΚΥΡΙΣ ΣΕΡβΑΝΔΟΣ ΑΙΠΟΙΗΘΕΝ),*

from which it might be inferred that it was the handiwork of one Servandus. 2. An inscription on the back
of the first leaf,[27] four words of which are manifestly
written on erasures (here distinguished by italics):—

"*Cenobium* ad eximii merito venerabile *Saluatoris*
Quem caput ecclesiæ dedicat alta fides
Petrus Langobardorum extremis de finib. abbas
Devoti affectus pignora mitto mei,
Meque meosq. optans tanti inter gaudia patris
In cælis memorem semper habere locum."

* *i.e.*, ὁ κυριος Σερβανδος ἐποιησεν = The master Servandus
executed [this work].

As the lines in which there are no erasures are regular hexameters and pentameters, it was clear that the erasures had marred both the metre and the sense. In two lines the metre was entirely destroyed. The Saviour is said to be "dedicated by lofty faith as the Head of the Church." True, certainly ; but unlikely to be enunciated in such a way. He is also called Father " tanti inter gaudia patris," which is still less to be expected. But the purport is quite clear. Peter, an Abbat in Lombardy, sends the volume to the venerable Monastery of the Saviour, and he alters the original inscription to suit his own purpose. The object, then, with enquirers was, if possible, to restore the original inscription, in doing which, of course, the metre was a most valuable guide. First, then, Bandini proposed to read the first line,

"Culmen ad eximii merito venerabile Petri."

This brought the metre right, and " Petri" agreed well with "caput ecclesiæ." Still, the third line stood sorely in need of mending, and Bandini, availing himself of the hint conveyed in the inscription at the end of the prologue to Leviticus, suggested " Servandus Latii" in place of " Petrus Langobardorum ;" and the volume was supposed to have been a gift to the Holy See from Servandus of Latium, whoever he might have been. Still, neither " Langobardorum " nor " Latii" suited the phrase " extremis de finibus," neither Lombardy nor Latium being far from Rome. It occurred to another distinguished Italian scholar, " the famous epigraphist and historian of the catacombs, G. B. de Rossi," that " extremis de finibus " pointed to England. He had become acquainted with the Venerable Bede's story of Ceolfrid intending one of his three Pandects of the new translation as a gift to the Pope. He therefore proposed for the third line,

"Ceolfridus Britonum extremis de finibus abbas."

This seemed to satisfy the metre, supposing the penultimate of "Ceolfridus" to be long, and "Britonum"
agreed with "extremis de finibus."

Conjecture had arrived at this stage when, in the
Guardian of February 16th last, there appeared a paper
from the Bishop of Salisbury calling attention to the
subject. "The interest of De Rossi's discovery," his
Lordship most truly said, "for all members of the English Church is startling." Still, the origin of the Codex
remained a mystery. Where was it written? How did
Ceolfrid become possessed of it? Benedict had made
five journeys to Rome, in the fourth of which he was
accompanied by Ceolfrid, and the Pandect of the old
translation had come from Rome. Did Ceolfrid's three
Pandects of the new translation come from Rome too?
It was certainly a curious process to carry back to Rome
as a gift to the Pope, a manuscript which a few years
before had been brought from Rome; but no better
supposition seemed to occur to anyone. Meantime
another correction of the inscription was suggested by
a Cambridge scholar, the Rev. G. F. Browne,*[28] who
pointed out that Ceolfrid was not in the least likely to
describe himself as a "Briton;" he noticed also that
the penultimate of Ceolfridus was most probably short
from the analogy of "Wilfridus" (Bede, *H. E.* v. 19).
He therefore, for "Britonum" in the third line, proposed to read "Anglorum."

"Ceolfridus Anglorum extremis de finibus abbas."

* Now Bishop of Bristol.

All this while a full and clear solution of the problem
was lying ready and close at hand in the anonymous
Life of Ceolfrid, with which, unfortunately, no one who
had yet taken part in the discussion seems to have been
acquainted. . They knew only the Venerable Bede's
Lives of the Abbats of Wearmouth and Jarrow. Speaking of the close of Ceolfrid's career, the anonymous
writer says :—

"He made noble additions to the library which either he
or Benedict had brought from Rome; inasmuch as, among
other things, he caused to be written three Pandects,
two of which he placed in the Churches of his two Monasteries, that if anyone wished to read any chapter of
either Testament he might readily find what he desired;
the third he proposed to offer as a gift to St. Peter, the
Prince of the Apostles, when he should take his journey
to Rome."[29]

Surely there could not be a more appropriate or ac-
ceptable gift than such a fair Codex, written in a remote
English Monastery.

Here, then, the origin of the great Codex is fully dis-
closed. It was written in the united Monastery at the
very time that the Venerable Bede was living, and studying, and teaching at Jarrow. This most important passage was pointed out, immediately after the Bishop of
Salisbury's appeal, by Dr. Hort,[30] Hulsean Professor
of Divinity at Cambridge, in a letter to *The Academy.*
But this is not all. St. Ceolfrid's biographer, after nar-
rating the circumstances of his departure from Wearmouth, his journey through France, and his death at
Langres, goes on to say[31] that some of his company
went on to Rome, bearing with them Ceolfrid's gifts,
"among which was the Pandect we spoke of, translated

by St. Jerome from the Hebrew and Greek originals, having at the beginning verses to this effect :—

> ' Corpus ad eximii merito venerabile Petri
> Dedicat ecclesiæ quem caput alta fides,
> Ceolfridus, Anglorum extimis de finibus abbas,
> Devoti affectus pignora mitto mei,
> Meque meosque optans tanti inter gaudia patris
> In cælis memorem semper habere locum.' "

With the exception of a transposition in the second line, and the form " extimis " for " extremis " in the third, these lines are identical with all that part of the inscription now to be seen in the Codex which has not suffered erasion. The inevitable inference is that they supply the true reading of the erased words. The slight discrepancies just mentioned might easily be caused by a lapse of memory in the writer ; in fact he only professes to give them " to this effect," " versus hujusmodi." It is most remarkable that the whole inscription except the first word, which now becomes " corpus " instead of " culmen," had been correctly restored by the learned ingenuity of modern Italian and English scholars, before attention was drawn to the anonymous *Life of Ceolfrid.* The inscription supplies *ex abundantia* the last link—a link perhaps scarcely required—in the chain of evidence. It is worth remarking, too, that, with one exception, the metre of the inscription in the Codex has now become faultless. The exception is that the second syllable of " ecclesiæ " is shortened. The same anomaly occurs repeatedly in Bede's metrical *Life of St. Cuthbert,* and in other of his poems. Greek scholarship was not then very extensive or accurate.[32] They used Greek words much as we now use the Hebrew when we speak of Lébanon, Chérubim, Séraphim, whereas those who are skilled in

the Hebrew tongue tell us that we ought to say Lebā-
non, Cherūbim, Serāphim. It is very far from unlikely
that this inscription was written by the Venerable Bede.
Does it even seem an extravagant stretch of fancy to
suppose that ĭt may be an autograph?

There cannot now be the least shadow of doubt that
this famous manuscript is the identical Pandect which
was intended by Abbot Ceolfrid as a gift to St. Peter,
and of course Servandus was relegated to the region
of shades. It is supposed that he may have been the
writer of the manuscript from which the Pandect was
copied, and that the scribe, who, though clearly a
master in calligraphy, may not after all have been a
very intelligent man, had simply copied what he found,
without regard to the fact that it was really no part of
the work.

There is still another point to which Dr. Hort has
directed attention. As far back as 1883 it was pointed
out by Dr. Peter Corssen, of Jever,[33] that there was
some close relationship between the *Codex Amiatinus*
and the three Latin Bibles described by Cassiodorus,[34]
as presented by him to his Monastery at Vivarium.
This eminent and excellent man had held various high
offices under Theodoric, the Ostrogothic King of Italy,
and at the age of 60 retired from public life to "spend
the remainder of his days in monastic seclusion."[35] He
survived 35 years, and "consecrated his old age to religious meditation and to a work even more important
than any of his political labours,—the preservation by
the pens of monastic copyists of the Christian Scriptures, and of the great works of classical antiquity."
Among other things he wrote a book for his monks,
called "Institutio Divinarum et Humanarum Literar-
um," in which he gives various lists of the sacred books,

and speaks of a representation of the Temple of Solomon, and of Ezra writing at a table, of which he gives a description. Now, the *Codex Amiatinus* contains similar lists of the sacred books, and also a representation of the Temple of Solomon and of Ezra writing at his table, so that little doubt is left that the preliminary matter of the Codex is derived directly or indirectly from Cassiodorus.

Amongst others of his Codices, Cassiodorus notices particularly one of the old translation, which he describes as "Codex grandior littera clariore conscriptus." In this he had caused the lists of the sacred books and the representation of the Temple of Solomon to be inserted. Now, it has been pointed out by Dr. Hort[36] that the Venerable Bede, in two of his expository works, mentions a representation of the Temple of Solomon in a Pandect of Cassiodorus, of which he speaks as one who had actually seen it.

In his tract on the Tabernacle, ii. 12 (vii. 107 of Giles), Bæda speaks as follows : " Quomodo in pictura Cassiodori Senatoris cujus ipse in expositione Psalmorum[37] meminit expressum vidimus ;" and again in his tract on Solomon's Temple, c. 16 (viii. 314 f. of Giles) : " Has vero porticus Cassiodorus Senator in Pandectis, ut ipse Psalmorum expositione commemorat, triplici ordine distinxit," adding below, " Hæc ut in pictura Cassiodori reperimus distincta."

But we have no reason to believe that Bede was ever in Italy, or, in fact, ever travelled further South than York. He must, therefore, have seen the Pandect of Cassiodorus at home, so that it is as nearly certain as can be that this was the Pandect of the old translation which Benedict or Ceolfrid brought from Rome. In course of time it had found its way from Vivarium to

Rome, where, after the new translation by St. Jerome came into favour, it might not be so highly prized, and had been acquired by Benedict in one of his numerous journeys. It would naturally be regarded with great reverence in Northumbria, and though Ceolfrid's Pandects were certainly not copied from it, seeing they were of a different translation, yet it is plain that the preliminary matter would be equally suitable to either version.

Thus this grand Codex, of which Dr. Hort says, " Even on a modern spectator this prodigy of a manuscript leaves an impression not far removed from awe," has been fairly traced to its birthplace in the united Monastery of Wearmouth and Jarrow. First, it was manifest that the inscription at the beginning was not in its original state ; part had been erased and new words written over the erasures. Then came the guess founded on the hint conveyed in the inscription at the end of the prologue to Leviticus, referring to Servandus. Next comes the persuasion that " extremis de finibus " fits neither Lombardy nor Latium in reference to Rome, and the most happy conjecture of G. B. de Rossi about St. Ceolfrid, founded on the Venerable Bede's *Lives of the Abbats,* which ultimately led to the restoration, still by conjecture, of every word but one of the original inscription. Then Dr. Hort directs attention to the passages in the anonymous *Life of St. Ceolfrid,* in which it is stated that Ceolfrid caused three Pandects of the new translation to be written, one of which he intended for the Pope ; and along with this to the original inscription itself, agreeing in every word but one with the conjectural restoration of the inscription now to be seen in the Codex, so that the origin and early history of " this prodigy of a manuscript " were removed from the region of doubt and conjecture into that of absolute certainty. Lastly we have Dr. Hort's identification of the Pandect of the old translation at Wearmouth with Cassiodorus's "Codex grandior littera clariore conscriptus." It is surely a most interesting and a most marvellous history.

There, then, were these three great manuscripts, the "Codex grandior" of the old translation in the library, and the two Pandects of the new, one in the Church of St. Peter and the other in the Church of St. Paul, in the ancient united Monastery. Dr. Hort thinks it would be "a wonder if these two huge manuscripts in the two famous Abbey Churches did not exercise a wide influence for centuries." Alas! it must be feared that their time was very brief. In little more than 70 years after the death of St. Ceolfrid came the first Danish invasion of Northumbria. Lindisfarne, Wearmouth, and Jarrow were sacked with circumstances of peculiar atrocity, and there can be little doubt that the "Codex grandior" of Cassiodorus, and the two Pandects of St. Ceolfrid were then destroyed. After that a long period of intellectual torpor and darkness succeeded in the North, indeed, in England generally. Let us rejoice that the third Pandect of St. Ceolfrid was far away in Italy, safe from the heathen ravager, and that it has remained to this day the admiration of all who behold it, to be a monument to the pious zeal and learning of the monks of Wearmouth and Jarrow, and their learned and holy Abbat, St. Ceolfrid.

NOTES.

1. *i.e.* of the whole Bible ; as to the New Testament, the Codex Fuldensis is older.

2. *Hist. Eccl.* iv. 18, v. 21, 24.

3. Bede's *Lives of the Abbats* is printed in Dr. Smith's edition of Bede's *Historical Works*, 1722 ; in the edition of the *Historical Works* published by the English Historical Society, edited by Joseph Stevenson, 1841 ; in the *Works of the Venerable Bede,* edited by Dr. Giles, 1843; in Hussey's edition of the *Hist. Eccl.,* 1846 [and separately, edited by the Rev. Peter Wilcock, 1910, published by Hills & Co., Sunderland].

4. The anonymous *Life of St. Ceolfrid* was first printed in the Appendix to the English Historical Society's edition of the *Historical Works,* from Harleian MS. No. 3020, and is reprinted by Dr. Giles in his Appendix. Mr. Stevenson asserts that it was the source from which the Venerable Bede derived much of his information for his *Lives of the Abbats.* It is difficult to understand how anyone acquainted with both *Lives* could say so. Mr. Stevenson seems to have been thinking of what is commonly said of Bede's *Life of St. Cuthbert,* and the anonymous *Life* by a monk of Lindisfarne. But the two cases are widely different. St. Cuthbert lived at a considerable distance from Jarrow, and died when Bede was very young. Bede spent all his life after the age of seven in the Monastery of Jarrow ; he must have been an eye and ear witness of most of what he sets down, and it is not easy to see what need he had for help from anyone in recording events of which he could most emphatically say, were he so inclined, "Quorum pars magna fui." All that he could not be acquainted with from personal knowledge is the early history of St. Benedict Biscop, of which the anonymous writer says nothing. On the other hand the latter gives a brief account of the early life of St. Ceolfrid, of which Bede says nothing. The anonymous *Life* has all the appearance of a sermon for the Natalitia of the Saint. The writer begins with a text, and a most appropriate one—Heb. xiii., 7, and his subject is St. Ceolfrid alone, others being mentioned only incidentally.

References are here made to the English Historical Society's edition. *B. H. E.*—Bede's *Ecclesiastical History ; B. V. A.* —Bede's *Lives of the Abbats ; V. A.*—Anonymous *Life of St. Ceolfrid.*

5. *Lives of the Saints,* September 25.

6. *V. A.* 318.

7. Ibid 331.

8. Ibid 318.

9. *V. A.* 319.

10. Ibid.

11. Benedict had really been *four* times at Rome. In his second journey he returned as far as Lérins, where he stayed some time and received the tonsure, and then went back to Rome. Bede reckons the journeys as "from Britain,"—"de Brittannia Romam." He made in all five journeys, or six according as the second from Britain, during which he was twice at Rome, is counted as one or as two.

12. *B. V. A.* 150; *V. A.* 320.

13. Ibid 143.

14. *V. A.* 320.

15. *B. V. A.* 143.

16. Since it was thus introduced by Benedict Biscop the manufacture of glass has been a leading industry on the spot. It is now fast retiring to Belgium. Was Belgium the part of Gaul from which Benedict fetched it?

17. *V. A.* 321.

18. *B. V. A.* 145; *V. A.* 322.

19. *V. A.* 323.

20. Bed. *Hist. Eccl.* v. 24.

21. *B. V. A.* 150; *V. A.* 323.

22. This is probably the first historical mention of *consumption*, as Montalembert remarks, "Le premier des Anglais, je pense, chez lequel l'histoire ait signalé cette maladie si habituelle et si fatale à leur race."—*Moines d'Occident*, iv. 485.

23. *B. V. A.* 150-154.

24. Ibid 155; *V. A.* 325.

25. Πανδεκτης, *all receiving, all containing*, hence οἱ Πανδεκται, name for a universal dictionary or encyclopædia; but later, the Pandects or General Code of Law, drawn up by order of Justinian (Liddell & Scott). They have overlooked its application to the Scriptures. But Maitland (*Dark Ages*, p. 194), was not aware of this use of the word so early:—"I do not know that this name [for the Scriptures] was ever general, or that it was used by any writer before Alcwin."

26. *The Guardian*, February 16; *Academy*, February 12.

27. A facsimile of this inscription will be found in the Palæo-graphical Society's publications, 2nd Series, part iv. pp. 65, 66. We take this opportunity of strongly commending this remarkable and "epoch-making" publication to the attention of our readers. Under the able auspices of Mr. Maunde Thompson, the distinguished Keeper of the Manuscripts in the British Museum, it has acquired a European reputation, and has given rise to similar undertakings in France, and, we believe, in Germany.

28. *The Guardian*, March 2.

29. *V. A.* 325.

30. *The Academy*, February 26.

31. *V. A.* 332.

32. In a verse of Alcwin's, quoted by the Bishop of Salisbury (*The Guardian*, February 16), we have a similar instance :—
    "Quod nunc a multis constat *Bibliotheca* dicta."

33. See the Bishop of Salisbury's paper in *The Guardian*, February 16, and Dr. Hort's paper in *The Academy*, February 26.

34. Always so named, until of late the spelling "Cassiodor*ius*" has come into favour. The history of this remarkable man has recently been illustrated most fully by Mr. Hodgkin in vol. iv. of *Italy and her Invaders,* a work in which evidence of the most laborious research is joined to a most attractive style, qualities which are not always found combined. Mr. Hodgkin has also published *The Letters of Cassiodorus* in a separate work, to which is prefixed a biography, in p. 5 of which the question of the spelling of the name is discussed. Mr. Hodgkin, for the present at least, prefers "Cassiodorus," and quotes an hexameter verse of Alcwin as evidence of the spelling in the eighth century. He might have added the Venerable Bede, only in this case prose is not such sure evidence as verse. Gibbon and Dr. Westcott in 1866 (*The Bible in the Church*) agree with Mr. Hodgkin. In such company we may be excused if we write "Cassiodorus."

35. Hodgkin, *Letters of Cassiodorus*, p. 54. See also the article on "Cassiodorus" in *C. Q. R.* for July, 1880, pp. 289-318.

36. *The Academy*, February 26.

37. It may be worth noting in connection with these passages that there is in the Cathedral Library at Durham, a manuscript of Cassiodorus's "Exposition of the Psalms," which tradition, perhaps not on very secure grounds, asserts to be the handiwork of the Venerable Bede himself.

APPENDIX II.

THE
GREENWELL LEAF AND THE WOLLATON MSS.

———

The very interesting account of the *Codex Amiatinus,* which we have been permitted to reproduce *in extenso,* reminds us of the statement made by our author (§ 20) that this great manuscript volume was not in the first instance unique. He tells us that Ceolfrid caused not one but three pandects to be written out, two of which were to remain, and no doubt long did remain, one in each of his monastic houses. That some portions at least of one or other of these copies might be surviving and possibly be recovered must have long been the desire of those who have read his words. This desire has in recent years been happily fulfilled.

The first known of the rescued fragments is described in the *Journal of Theological Studies* for July, 1909 (Vol. x., No. 40, pp. 540-544). Mr. C. H. Turner relates how he saw and examined this MS. in Canon Greenwell's house at Durham. The owner had picked it up some twenty years before in a bookseller's shop at Newcastle. It had been folded in two to form the cover of an account book, dating about the year 1780. He observed at once its resemblance to the *Codex Amiatinus,* of which, however, it formed no part; but, as Canon Greenwell suggested, it was undoubtedly a portion of one of the sister volumes. The size of the leaf is 48 by 34 centimetres; that of the *Codex* being 50 by 34 centimetres. There are, as in that manuscript, two columns to the page, the number of lines in each being

44. The writing is not that of the same scribe, but in a somewhat smaller hand, and the writer has made use of more contractions of final syllables and letters. The first lines of the capitula are in each coloured red. The contents of the leaf are the new or Jerome's Latin version of the Old Testament, Third (First) Book of Kings, xi. 29—xii. 18. A scribe of the fourteenth (or possibly thirteenth) century has substituted the figure xii. for xiii. in the margin at the beginning of the twelfth chapter. The recovered leaf has since been presented by Canon Greenwell to the British Museum.

It is a pleasure to be able to relate that considerable further portions of the same manuscript have quite recently come to light. These are in the library of Lord Middleton at Wollaton, Nottinghamshire, and are carefully described in the Report of the Historical Manuscripts Commission for 1911 (pp. 196 and 611). They consist of ten leaves, which have been used to form covers for chartularies of the various Willoughby estates, drawn up in the early part of the sixteenth century, and bound not earlier than the reign of Edward VI. The portions of Scripture which they contain are III. Kings, xxi. 17—IV. Kings iii. 25 ; IV. Kings viii. 27—x. 19 ; xv. 12—xvi. 6 ; xvi. 20—xvii. 15 ; xviii. 36—xix. 31 ; and xxi. 6—xxii. 13. To quote the Report : — "They agree with the Greenwell Leaf in the size of the parchment, the size and arrangement of the columns and lines, the handwriting, the ruling, the absence of punctuation, the character of the headline, 'Malachim' (= Kings), its position on the page and its occurrence only on the right side of each leaf, the writing of the first line of each chapter in red, the rubrication (even to the alteration of the chapter numbers in a later hand, and the character of the ruled lines in red, indicating the position of the number in the text)." A footnote describes these alterations as being probably the work of a thirteenth century scribe, who has also written between the two books of Kings the words " Explicit Regum liber tertius. Incipit liber quartus " (= End of the third book of Kings; beginning of the fourth book).

It will be observed that the first of these ten leaves is quite a near neighbour to that discovered by Canon Greenwell. How this portion of this particular *Codex* found its way into Nottinghamshire some antiquary may possibly tell us. They may, we hope, have the good fortune to be reproduced as the single leaf has now been by the new Palæographical Society. (Plates 158, 159.)

D. S. B.

[The writer's thanks are due to Mr. W. H. Stevenson, St. John's College, Oxford, for reference to his report on the Wollaton MSS.]

INDEX.

(The numbers given indicate the page; those in heavy type —i.e. pp. 55-88—refer to *The Life of Ceolfrid.*)

Eosterwini, abbot at Wearmouth, 2, 31, 48, 61, 63, 64, 66, 68, 99, 100
Escomb church, 43
Ezra, 108

FINAN, bishop of Lindisfarne, 20
Finees. *See* Phinehas
Florence, Mediceo - Laurentian Library at, 40, 95, 101, 102
Fresca, river (unidentified), 91

GANGWULF, 83, 85, 92
Gaul (now France), 20, 58, 60, 79, 80, 99
Gibbon, the historian, 113
Gilling (Yorkshire), monastery at, 10, 20, 23, 24, 56, 97
Glass, art of making, brought to England, 99, 112
Gregory II., pope, 50, 77
    letter of 51, 85, 87
Greenwell, Rev. Canon, 114-116
    Leaf, The, 4, 114, 115
Guardian, The, 104, 113

HEAVENFIELD, battle of, 5
Hebrews, Epistle to the 55
Heptarchy, the Saxon, 5
Hexham, 5, 20
Hilda, St., abbess, 20
Hilperic (= Chilperic II.), King of Neustria, 80, 92
Hort, Rev. Dr., 105, 107-110
Humber, river, 79
Hwaetbercht, abbot of Wearmouth and Jarrow, 2, 50, 76, 85, 91
    letter of, 77

IKANHOE (now Boston), 97
Indictions (the term explained), 89
Iona, island and monastery, 13, 20, 22, 27, 36
Islands, The (i.e. Lérins), 58, 89
Ireland, 9, 10, 23, 25, 56
Ireland and the Celtic Church, 25

JARROW, monastery and churches at, 17, 21, 29, 32, 41-44, 48, 100, 105. *See also* St. Paul's, and Wearmouth and Jarrow
Jerome, St., 84, 95, 106
John (of Beverley), bishop of Hexham, 21
John the chanter, 21, 29, 62, 99
Joshua, 87
Justinian, the emperor, 91, 112

KENT, 20, 57, 97
Kings, books of, 115

LANCASHIRE, battle at Maserfield in, 5
Land of families (term explained), 90
Langres (Burgundy), 80, 83, 85, 101, 105
Laurence, St., oratory of 42, 73
Leeds, 5
Leonella, martyr, 84
Lérins, 89
Leviticus, Book of, 102
Lives of the Abbots. See Bede
Life of Ceolfrid. See Ceolfrid, *Life of*
Lindisfarne, 19, 20, 110
Lindbrand, king of the Lombards, 80
Lombardy, Lombards, 80, 103
Low, Rev. J. L., 4, 40
    article and notes by, 95-113

MAITLAND, quoted, 112
Martin's, St., Rome, 62
Master-builders brought by Biscop from Gaul, 60
Meliosippus, martyr, 84
Memorials of Old Durham, 45
Mercia, Mercians, 5, 19
Merovingian dynasty, 92
Middleton, Lord, 115
Monastery of St. Peter and St. Paul, 1, 17. *See also* Wearmouth and Jarrow
Monastery of the Saviour, 103
    See also Gilling, Iona, Ripon
Monasticism, 9-13
Monkwearmouth, 41-44, 48. *See also* Wearmouth
Montalembert, quoted, 112
Monte Amiata, 101, 102
Moses, 59, 87
Music, 15, 18, 29, 62

NAITON, King, 21, 33, 36
Nechtansmere (Dumfries), battle of, 5, 16, 21
Neustria, 92
Newcastle, 114
Northumbria, Northumbrians, 1, 3, 5, 7, 21-22, 39
    Christianity of, 8
Nursia (Italy), 11, 91